525

FLYING SAUCER

FLYING SAUCER

Gurdjieff Revisits Earth

This is a crazy book! It claims to be about communications from Gurdjieff since his death. They come from observation and following his *Advice of Grandmother:* "or do nothing, just go to school, or do something no one else does". But it feels as if many people and happenings contributed. There is more in the kitchen. Sorry, no *bon ton* literary finish.

The cover photograph is of a wood carving *"The Craftsman's Hands"* by Professor M. W. Thring.

Flying Saucer

Gurdjieff Revisits Earth

Brynhild Wooldridge Thring

Coombe Springs Press

ISBN 0 900306 52 1

Coombe Springs Press
Daglingworth Manor
Daglingworth
Nr. Cirencester
Gloucestershire

CONTENTS

CONTENTS (continued)

CONTENTS (continued)

References to books used are:

All and Everything, or ***Beelzebub's Tales to His Grandson (A&E)*** Published by Routledge and Kegan Paul, 1950

Meetings with Remarkable Men (R.M.) Routledge and Kegan Paul 1963.

Also P. D. Ouspensky, ***In Search of the Miraculous, Fragments of an Unknown Teaching,*** 1949

G. R. S. Mead, ***Thrice-Greatest Hermes,*** Watkins, 1906, 1964.

Glamour photograph taken by Lucien Myers on one of the Bennett holidays at Langdale Estate in 1944 and 1945. Secret ''movements'' in the squash court. The 1945 holiday received the shock news of the Hiroshima bomb. 1946 was the first Coombe Springs Seminar.

I

FLYING SAUCER: GURDJIEFF REVISITS EARTH

THIS STORY IS FICTION and no one is to pretend it happened like this. On a bright autumn morning in the forest near a collective farm in Siberia, a woodcutter heard a roll of thunder; suddenly with a rushing wind a dazzling orange flying saucer landed in a clearing. A hatch opened up, and out climbed two beings in the shape of men, one short, square and dark, the other tall, willowy and fair.

The woodcutters were frightened, but the Saucer Men spoke to them in Russian in a friendly way, saying they had been sent to earth with a message. By good fortune the party bosses had just gone away for a conference, and work was slack after the potato harvest, so the foresters agreed to tell the other villagers. As everyone had heard the thunder-clap it was not long before an exited and curious crowd gathered round the saucer.

The two strangers climbed on its roof. The short one held up his hand for silence, and began: ''We have come specially to show you that dying is not the end of life, for we ourselves have died and you see we are quite alive. The message has been sent before, but now too many people no longer believe in a life after death, or that *how* you live on earth makes all the difference to being happy or unhappy in the next world.''

Born in Armenia, he had spent his earthly life first in the search to understand the meaning of man's life and its relation to the Higher Powers, and afterwards to training people to reach their own understanding. His companion had been a follower of the teachings. He died at 42, apparently rejected and a failure, by falling from a hotel fire-escape in Wellington, New Zealand, in a high wind while watching for the American satellite Echo, a silvered balloon. It was September 2nd or 3rd, 1960, almost exactly 21 years after Hitler's invasion of Poland. His death was a sacrifice, because he was needed as a pilot for this mission, which cost other lives too.

"Won't you tell us what it is like to be dead?" asked an old man.

"I can't really do that, for it is beyond anything you have experienced. Dying has to remain a great adventure into the unknown – perhaps a dangerous adventure that should be well prepared,

"But I will tell you a way of thinking about it. Dying is like labour pains, bringing to birth an invisible body formed during life, made out of actions and character, memories, sufferings, right thoughts, relations with other people, things made and cared for, all that you loved, all that you truly learned.

"People who live rightly are reborn with strong healthy heavenly bodies; they find friends and relations waiting to welcome them and help them start a new life. But people who lead selfish lives, whether actual crime, or dominating their families, or making use of other people, or as emotional parasites, are likely to be born blind, crippled or worse, and there may not be anyone who wants to help them. If someone whose earthly body is handicapped does not pity himself but achieves an inner independence, he earns a specially beautiful resurrection body in compensation.

"You must not die before it is the right time for you to go, or you might find yourself like a bird with only one wing, unable to fly – for some of us can fly, and can see you, though you cannot ordinarily see us."

At this the pilot threw his own trilby and the Teacher's astrakhan cap high into the air, leaped up himself and flew round the clearing chasing the hats, like the American Superman with his raincoat billowing. Finally he turned head over heels, bounced off the Teacher's shaven head and landed neatly beside him, bowing as he politely returned the cap amidst general laughter.

The Teacher went on: "Beyond the individual level these bodies are also, as it were, cells in the growing body of "All Humanity", "All Life on Earth" or the "Cosmic Christ", the Son of the High

Universal God that Mother Earth is producing. Like a human body, the Great Body needs many kinds of cells – muscle, bone, nerve, brain, gland – but it needs them healthy and able to fulfil their particular function. If the cells achieve their destiny, they are both *separate,* remaining themselves, and ***united*** into the collective mind and will."

"Where in all the vast universe is this home of the dead?" the old man asked.

"It is really close at hand. Ask the best physicists. They know the limitations of your perceptions of space and time."

The peasants listened willingly, for they were tired of scienfific materialism, so the visitors said they would stay a few days and hold more conversations.

* * * * * * *

The next day was Saturday, but they could not have a general meeting till late afternoon because the younger men were football fans and must listen to the big match. Then the Teacher said: "That is another way of picturing the life of the dead. We join a team, the team of the Angels, working together on God's plans. We can influence the world of time and space. Any of you can turn to the Angels and feel you have friends who care, and can help in times of difficulty. For us this working together as a team is a great joy. Maybe the Angel's colours should be yellow and blue for the sun and sky," he finished with a smile.

"And yellow stands for hope," declared the pilot, for it was his favourite colour. "Our life is also like dancing to music," he added. He himself had given much pleasure by his gift for piano playing.

"Yes," the Teacher went on, "but none of these analogies must be pushed too far, or made into dogma that fetters minds. Human thinking and human words can never catch a whole reality, only one aspect at a time. One-sided statements can be dangerous if acted on, as for instance in child psychology. Balance, avoiding extremes, is harder to express, so controversy and debate are useful if they are not just angry obstinacy. In this you can say 'Love your enemies' to the extent of learning from them, and as a stimulus."

"Is there an enemy team of real Devils?" objected one of the keen footballers. "Do people dying with bitterness and grudges have the power to hurt us?"

"This is one of the questions which are really beyond ordinary words and thinking; or perhaps it is unbearable to admit that He whom we call God may be behind our suffering. There are many devils – ignorance, blind mechanicalness, complacency and laziness, verbal wise-acring, besides cruelty, envy and intolerance . . . and it is right to fight against them, ***first of all,*** inside yourselves. Whether there is a Master Devil and a universal struggle between good and evil, as some have taught, I can't answer.

"It seems likely the many devils are part of the conditions of material existence and the competition for survival in physical bodies, out of which spirits must be created; but the Master Devil is really God in disguise, taking advantage of the negative forces, 'All things work together for good for them that love God', in the end, in the very long run!

"You cannot defeat the insidious powers of evil by force, and more force. First put your own house in order, cast out the beam from your own eye. Then perhaps a way will be shown for hearts and minds to change."

(To be honest, George Gurdjieff's answer in his own book ***All and Everything*** is to make Beelzebub a being who has achieved a high degree of reason, but not the highest, since his exile for the youthful sin of pride.)

"What should we do now?" asked one of the young people.

"You must choose. Decide for yourselves which way your life shall go. This is the right kind of egoism. Aim to live so that in the next world you could face a Judge who cannot be cheated, and show that you did your best with the talents and circumstances that were given you.

"Try to live as good neighbours. The old Golden Rule still stands. Kindness, courage, cheerfulness, honesty, forgiveness – you do know the things that are good. But to pursue them you must have self-knowledge, awareness of your actual behaviour.

"Observe yourselves impartially, your movements, postures, moods, associations, impulses. Observe also others, observe the flow of events (easy or frustrating), coincidences, the growth of plants, the flavour of food, the weather.

"Observe the spontaneous acts of animals and children, for of such is the kingdom of heaven – but adults have in addition the responsibility of keeping a critical watch on *their* spontaneity. Things too can teach you, about their quality and durability, the associations they arouse, and even the ingenious ways they lose themselves and turn up again (ascribed to gremlins in war-time R.A.F. stations).

"Attention is the force available to you for work. Have a target for it. When you 'come to' and notice it has strayed to day-dream or imaginary conversation, put aside the distraction and bring attention back. For exercise to stretch attention, divide it, for example between what you are doing and sensing your hand, or between the person you are talking to and listening to your voice.

"Practice relaxing your limbs; then noticing tension can be a reminding 'interruption' to the automatic flow. Cultivate sensible habits. Apply 'time and motion study' to your chores.

"Experiment, do things differently; use the other hand, walk faster or slower, choose your sitting positions, stand more upright. See how posture expresses and affects mood, from thumb-sucking onwards.

"Try this for three months; each evening find one new thing that you learned during the day. Write it down if you like. 'If you like' – you must be able to do things you don't like, but observe the likes too, they can be a guide to what you really want (excitement, praise, affection, a Rock of Security?).

"The way to die well is to live well, to use the 'now' fully, for time never stops running away with your years. 'Use the present to repair the past and prepare the future.' And remember your own dead, both relations and older friends."

* * * * * * *

On Sunday the schoolmaster, an older man who listened to foreign news broadcasts in secret, asked about the world's practical problems – overpopulation, the rape of nature, crime and terrorism, financial greed, the threats of war, abuse of political power, bribery and corruption, hypocrisy and the prostitution of language for advertisement and propaganda, exploiting even compassion.

"The problems are indeed grave", said the Teacher. "Do not be misled by people who promise a wonderful future in Time if you follow them. Each generation knots its own section of the great carpet, or writes its own chapter of the big book, that is the earth's history. The achievements and sufferings of past generations are still real, preserved in the earth's memory, and count as much as the present which must add its own contribution, or the future which always brings some unforeseen factors. You cannot know the plan for the future but those who wish to help may watch for hints of what to do next, using caution and trained attention.

"One thing that is needed is a different attitude to community, to death and the invisible world, which is why we were sent with this message. From such a change of attitude much else could follow. The true socialism is the wish to serve, however humbly, the whole Great Society of Planet Earth on both sides of the one-way-looking-glass curtain of death, but to do this you must also grow yourselves.

"Your first duties are to those nearer to you, your family, your village, your own home country, but they should be loving services, given willingly by free individuals, not a tyranny and not ***against*** other groups beyond the limits of sporting competition. People should be valued by their usefulness and not their numbers alone; by their inner qualities and character more than by possessions and success. Riches should be held as a trust, to be used responsibly and not for undue luxury. Do not envy the rich, they are sent other kinds of suffering.

"If you see cruelty and injustice or stupidity among the power-possessors, condemn the conduct but try not to hate the people for that warps you. If they make bad karma it will take effect for them in the end, unless redeemed; but if you behave as badly as your enemies, do you deserve to win?

"In society as in a house the dirt never stops coming, you must keep on cleaning. Even the most useful institutions go wrong from human failings; vigilance must be renewed. Start by trying to teach the children that violence, stealing and lying will spoil their own future. Teach them by example and explanation the laws of physical and psychological health.

"But the Lord works in a mysterious way. History has always been full of tragedies and sufferings. All sheep must be shorn. Everyone must yield up energies for the cosmic purposes, but you can try to work so that you will earn 'treasure in heaven' to show for having lived, and also perhaps minimise the need for sacrifices."

"You spoke about us choosing", said the schoolmaster, "but does humanity as a whole also have a choice to make? It certainly looks at the moment as if humanity had reached a point where it could quickly destroy itself."

"There is something in what you say", answered the Teacher. "In what way can a whole country or a large section of humanity make a choice? It can only be through choice by a sufficient number of individuals together with a sense of responsibility among those who lead opinion, and an attitude of asking us for help and guidance in matters beyond your own powers. But there is a ***price*** for help."

"What is the money that pays for help?"

"The payment is intelligent work and accepting suffering when it can't be avoided.

"Even when the activists are determined to choose wrong and lead people astray, and others persist in shortsightedness, being wrongly educated, all who love the same beliefs and sincerely try to follow the Good Examples are linked, and will be together in the next world, whatever the future on earth or the fate of those whose hearts are hardened against the Redemptive Stream (which your right work helps to swell)."

* * * * * * *

During the week the visitors went about the village in the daytime and watched the collective farm-hands at work. They praised the best work in handcrafts still practised, woodcarving, cross-stitch embroidery. "If a man can mend shoes ***well***, I can teach him." They did not forget the children, telling fairy stories, puns and jokes to them, for the Teacher loved to laugh; but he could also be frighteningly serious, making one's self-centred worries and inner noise feel shamefully trivial. He seemed to be begging people to see the gravity of their situation before it was too late.

The Teacher had an almost magical insight into people, acquired partly through his medical training, (But healing the body and prolonging life is not enough, the soul or psyche must also be healed by finding a meaning to life). He showed many of the villagers things about themselves they would never have admitted before, or gave them clues for meeting their personal problems. (Mr. Gurdjieff intrigued his students by teaching that when you have seen and understood your chief weakness or fault, it becomes you chief strength. "Chief feature" may be an indication of type (dictionary: Greek *tupos*, a blow, stamp) an idea he never explained clearly. Perhaps he really meant "God's Will" for the individual life, liable to show itself in the "blows of fate". Do not submit too easily. Jacob wrestled with the Angel all night in his tent).

"For young people work must start with the body," the Teacher said, so in the early evenings he gave them, in the former church, classes in yoga postures to practise on their own, for a few minutes when they got up each morning, (but see the caution in his chapter Ekim Bey) and taught a few of his own "movements" to be done with bodily awareness. Learning these was found acutely "attention stretching". He explained that if he called "Stop!" they must freeze everything instantly, posture, tensions, gaze, as far as possible thoughts, until he called "Enough". If they fell it was his responsibility. This exercise recalls Socrates' daimon whose intervention always took the form of stopping him from what he was doing.

Afterwards the visitors met with groups crammed into one or other of the little wooden houses; some still had a lamp burning before an ikon in the corner. They heard observations and answered questions, and then spoke about further topics; the birth of Christianity, the secret elements common to many religions, and symbolism in art and literature, and again about the other, cruel face of God, or how time itself may be an aspect of his power, as Father Time, the Merciless Heropass, continually impregnating Material Nature, driving her to higher creation – but these things remained elusive. The Teacher gave hints about parts of his early life which had intentionally been disguised in his published writings.

* * * * * * *

On the following Sunday the Teacher said: "Tomorrow we must leave you". He gave them some practical directions and added: "You can consult the schoolmaster privately. He has a good understanding and I have had special late-night talks with him; but do not forget he will also need some peace!

"I told you the Angels have the means to watch and to help people who want to grow. Remember our visit and, as it were, turn to us and call. The help may come in ways that you do not expect. 'Through the Unconscious you can be connected with anything in the universe, even God' (and also the dead; but the Unconscious is a Trickster, be cautious). 'Seek and you will find' is also sometimes a surprisingly good promise. But I cannot say that it will be all 'Roses, roses'."

The peasants were used to a hard life, so this did not frighten them, but they knew that anyone who tried to pass the message on to others would be persecuted and they were not brave enough for that. Could anything be done? There was a simple-minded youth whom no one took much notice of; he said he did not mind what happened to him and would do what he could if the two men would guide his speech.

"Tonight we will have a feast," the Teacher then announced. It was his "birthday", that is to say the anniversary of his death, October 29th, 1949.

A firepit was dug in the clearing and piles of wood collected and chopped. Pigs were trussed on spits for roasting and cauldrons of red beet soup set on to boil. Back in the village the women and girls baked fancy breads and chopped raw salad. Everyone worked with a will and the preparations seemed to go on oiled wheels.

It was late before all was ready. Then, warmly wrapped in coats and scarves, they gathered by moonlight round a splendid bonfire. The visitors brought out bottles of a delectable drink from the Saucer and the Teacher directed the pilot to tell a toast.

"To everyone we love, dead, living and not yet born", he said.

Then they both started carving the pigs, lit by lanterns and flaming brushwood, while the borshch was served. Each portion of meat was covered by a second plate to keep the heat in. Everyone had almost more than he could eat.

The Teacher entertained them with mimicry and his oft-told stories. He twirled up the corners of his moustache and he was a dapper Frenchman; he pulled them down and he was a Chinese sage.

"Why you look at me like cow, like cow on 'nouvelle peinte porte'?" he asked a woman. "Every day cow went into the forest on her own to graze. Once while she was out her master repainted the stable door. When she came home she could not recognise her 'porte'. 'My door white, not red' cow said; she shook her head and retraced her steps into the forest."

"I hope to recognise the door", the woman said.

"That needs much study. For now, better to look like little dog, like dog on stick – all excitement when Master takes his stick to go for walk. But it is also 'stick with which educated', so dog is not quite sure."

Presently the Teacher said, "Angels are too busy praying, trying to become Archangels". He lifted up his hands to right and left, "Wah, wah, wah," the Angels singing. "But Devil, he cavalier, he help."

When it was time for dessert, "Yong people make chain", the Teacher called. He did some magic with his hands and conjured luscious fresh peaches from the air, passing them to the pilot and so from hand to hand along the chain till everyone was served. Afterwards the Teacher played his own haunting music on a Greek hand organ, a type of concertina or squeeze box.

It was all an unforgettable experience, coming at the end of the extraordinary nine days, heightened by the visitors' impending departure, and gave those present a feeling of union and brotherhood to face the uncertain future. When everything was cleared away there was little time left for sleep.

Meanwhile the party bosses had heard a report of unusual happenings from a spy and were hurrying back early from the conference, bringing police and armoured cars.

On Monday morning the strangers said good-bye to the peasants and many of them were walking to the clearing when the cavalcade of armoured cars appeared down the road. The police scrambled out and advanced in a semi-circle, hands on holsters. As they got alarmingly near the pilot turned quickly and whipped out a small gun. Suddenly everyone found himself groping alone in a dense white mist. A chorus of laughter was heard. The mist soon cleared but there was no sign of the strangers or the Saucer, only a strong smell of garlic in the air. Every single policeman was seen to be furiously scratching his left knee but the villagers did not dare laugh at THEM. Black clouds covered the sun, a squally wind blew up and presently the first snow began to fall.

Distinctly shaken, the bosses called the police officers into a committee and finally agreed on a cover-up story to tell *their* bosses.

The youth had already set off for another village where he had relatives. He was able to carry the message to several neighbouring villages through underground contacts before the authorities caught up with him and shut him in the asylum. This did not stop the rumours of the visit of the flying saucer, which continued to circulate through the markets and villages of the forest and the steppe.

A few of the original hearers did take the development of an active and intelligent resurrection body, psyche or 'wedding garment' as a serious aim. They began to see the hindrances or negative states to be avoided in themselves, and how undue self-satisfaction and self-blame both feed the insensitive *false-self* or vanity. Perhaps from such people an influence may spread.

An old advertising slogan: "Pardon me, inner cleanliness comes first"; another: "Not too little, not too much", and "Do it yourself".

* * * * * * *

II

ARGUMENTS AND ADDITIONS

1. The "I" and Resurrection

Gurdjieff did not want slavish followers, but people who could act from their own"I" and hold to a purpose of their own, not just react as a legion of passing responses. Yet who can say what "I" really is? It touches on mystery. "I am" is a name of God. Did G mean us to think of this when he told us to say "I am"?

Walking down the road with free attention you can seem to have Ouspensky's double ended arrow <———>, an awareness of physical presence in your body, *and* of the world outside it. Then you find yourself at the baker without your purse. Why is that? Consciousness lit up one part of the room (the brain), but there had been darkness in the part that keeps track of what has to be done, at the critical time of getting ready to leave home.

There are the ups and downs of feeling: states of faith and affirmation, of reaching out; others that are black or grey (but may be paying for a bright one tomorrow). The "I" must persist through and come to recognise both, praying to make good use of the sunshine state, seeing the depression as physical and waiting for it to pass; or confronting the doubts with the memory of faith – it is not the world that has changed.

In a negative state of anger, or when physical security is threatened, there can be a strong feeling of "I": this must be physiology, the flow of adrenalin and the body's will to survive.

The "I" must use the possibilities of this period of the day, this season of the year, even if it is only "doing the next thing" or occupying the time. Play and relaxation, hobbies, also, have their place. "Patience is the mother of Will. If you haven't a mother, how can you be born?"

The real "I" would seem to lie in will, show itself in act. Behaviour must come from inside, and not just be pretending, priggishness, from the desire to win approval. That "I" takes time to grow, by inner struggle to keep upright, to hold on to an orientation. According to the accounts Gurdjieff hurried it by teasing his pupils into emotional storms of great intensity, but one supposes he, a mid-wife of souls, knew how much they could stand, or was under a guidance which knew.

For the rest of us, life itself does bring different sorts of testing times and emotional conflicts. ''Exams'' may end with student days, but some get matrimonial problems, others economic, or illness, not to mention troubles on a larger scale, war, revolution, natural disasters, strikes, slumps. Like Toynbee's civilisations, people, if they are to grow, need challenge, not too little, not too much. Bereavements and the facing of old age must come to all in the natural course of life.

What of the times of difficulty when we nearly gave up, but are afterwards so thankful we didn't, or not for too long? What saved us and got us to turn the corner? An ''I'' of habits built in past struggles, the support of friends, 'grace' from the intangible nowhere, the feeling that a child needs you?

Ouspensky's formulation of one of the goals of work as ''permanent I'' seems misleading. One must not look for static permanence, though one does hope there may be something lasting underlying all the fluctuations. Side by side with the idea of developing an ''I'' is the contrary idea of ''seeing one's own nothingness''. In this age of blowing one's own trumpet humility as the central Christian virtue is out of fashion and yet it is what makes one open and receptive, attentive. Failure in spite of efforts can be good for us, and exalted states, dangerous. Pride goes before a fall.

How is it that new ideas arise at times of unconsciousness, dressing, in water-closet, washing up at the sink, or by association from a dream? Ernest Bevin told Churchill he got such wonderful ideas while cleaning his own boots. (Another Winston Churchill wartime story reports that he told of a ship that was a total loss ''and believe it or not, the only wreckage left afloat was a door with my initials on it''). We hear ourselves say something with a further meaning which only strikes us later, whether useful or embarrassing. Children sometimes say such significant things: ''Where is my birthday now?'' ''What a pity the plane did not go even higher, we might have seen God'' ''Why do the baddies do bad things?''

Whence come sensations that do not seem to have a proper physical cause? Is not insanity really a kind of demonic possession, through this famous ''Unconscious'' or ''Unknown''? (Keep the unconscious clean. Do not feed it on cheap rubbish, excuses and resentments.) It would seem there can be inside us an emptiness which is one of the ''black holes'' through which the Unseen acts on our world.

''Play conscious role without identification''. Let your outside behave as appropriately as it can, while the inside keeps watch and makes adjustments as well as it can. It does not seem possible to avoid approving and disapproving of oneself (super-ego?) like Alice, alternately shooting up and shrinking, but both are warnings that one is asleep, not present.

A person just cannot have been here this morning, and have come to a complete end, be non-existent, this afternoon. The Creator is not so wasteful, or so one hopes. Yet it seems this so various and fluctuating ''I'' could not survive as an entity without a vehicle and its own structure of experience and memory.

Why did the ambiguous wording ''the body's will to survive'' present itself above? One feels so strongly about the body's growing old, about the universal and inevitable tragedy of ''never again'', that the meaning must be that the sacrifice of the body is not in vain. We must grow a heavenly body to continue as individuals, otherwise each consciousness, each bit of ''I'' would just be fused again into the general consciousness, the Great ''I'' or Great Self, and nothing would be gained by actualising the potential of each separate life. It does imply making good use of the body while you have it, do not abuse it. ''Know ye not that your body is the temple of the Holy Ghost which is in you'', I Corinthians 6.19.

Resurrection as the standing up again of the same material atoms of our physical bodies, out of the graves at some future Second Coming in Time, seems so manifestly absurd that we overlook the importance of the idea that we do need a ''Resurrection of the body '' – a body of finer matters which this bit of ''I'' can inhabit after death, able to play a part in the work of the next level. It may be that privation, pain and body's total surrender at death are sacrifices that transfer subtle matter over into other dimensions. Mr. Gurdjieff promised chapters in his "Third Series" on the physical, the astral and the divine bodies of man, so there are grounds for attributing to him a sermon on a Resurrection Body.

Tammuz, Attis, Adonis, the dying and resurrecting God, is an old and evidently well-loved idea in the Middle East, typified by the Sun, the annual cycle of vegetation, and the phallus, image of the male organ or member. To use the word resurrection for the life after death is perhaps etymologically incorrect but to our ears it carries the feeling of hope and of joy out of suffering.

The Christian church is said to have inherited the doctrines of the resurrection of the body from the East, and the immortality of the soul from Plato and the Greeks, and to have kept both. Here it is held that man is not born with a soul (psyche); this is something he has to acquire by living, and it does have a bodily organised element. What man is born with, is what is called by Gurdjieff the Essence.

It sounds unfair to those who die young and there must be an answer. Some did live more vividly in fewer years. Perhaps the formative first half of life is the most crucial, further development can continue in either world. If children die, perhaps the essence goes on with the family. Wouldn't heaven be dull without children and some animals?

2 Action of Theos

The name of God is a convenient shorthand as well as a profanity. We should not be too sure we know what it means. Gurdjieff once told Orage his "whim" was to bring a new understanding of God to the earth. Did he mean just a renewal of faith, or a different emphasis in theology as well? Could this be "All Ancestors" with "the Inner Circle of Humanity" and "the Angelic Host", forming "HEAVEN" or the nearest tier of divinity for our own earth, like our own blue atmosphere shown on the astronauts' photographs from space?

H.G. Wells, lecturing on World Brain on the brink of war, got his dimensions wrong. The world brain is not "of this world" in time and space, or in universities as we know them, though there are university people who contribute to it. Teilhard de Chardin's noosphere suggests a region of divinity local for our own earth. With the hugeness of space revealed by astronomy we do need such a localised concept.

Ancestor worship is one of the oldest human attitudes to the invisible power, and does still have something to contribute, though to draw the line between faith and superstition is not easy. It is not suggested we should put out honey or wheaten cakes for the dead, but it is felt they are not only "alive" but also still collectively active in our affairs, and that it is good for us to remember them.

In private thinking the short-hand for this aspect of divinity is "they" – or more respectably a "theos" for this earth; other names are the spirits, or the collective unconscious; heaven seems a good name. Perhaps one should say it is only the dead who have passed through their Purgatory (sometimes in this life?) who are thus "eaten by God" or become actively part of Him. Definition is dangerous, for ordinary thinking should be humble before such questions, and yet one goes on trying.

"Come, you little garlic-head, think! If spirits can really tap with the leg of a table it means that they have some physical force. And if they have, why should they resort to such an idiotic and moreover complicated means of communicating with people as tapping with the leg of a table? Surely they could transmit whatever they wished to say either by touch or by some other means." (Father Borsh in Gurdjieff's ***Meetings with Remarkable Men***. p. 61)

"They" would seem to act on our world through very small forces, which can accumulate in one direction; such could be putting an impulse into our heads or arousing associations; affecting sensations and health of organisms, the wearing out and the breaking of things, the aim of a bomb or a bullet, the timing which produces "chance, accidents, coincidences". Falling in love and the conception of children, selecting the particular semen and egg which carry heredity suitable for "their" plans, would seem one place where very small physical force can have a big effect in human history; a similar action would be the all-important mutations in the right direction for evolving new species in geological history.

One is inclined to feel that if "they" want to, they can build up or direct the forces that produce exceptionally hot, cold, dry or wet stormy, weather, or earthquakes in the earthquake region; possibly Ice Ages. So it is not impossible that "unbecoming behaviour" on a large scale could encourage punishment by natural disasters, and right living help to avert them. But one certainly must not say that any actual disaster is a punishment earned by the particular people who suffer it; they cannot be any more wicked than the rest of us.

In fact one feels more that disasters are part of a toll of sacrifice exacted to allow for benevolent interferences. Perhaps "they" have to balance favourable against unpleasant interventions, good luck against bad luck, and the ratio may not be one to one. If the cooking apple tree prospers strikingly the desert apple tree refuses to do so despite care. Illness as well as cures may be "miraculous". Miracles are expensive, someone somewhere has to pay.

This attitude may sound like "primitive animism," – mana or spirits, often hostile, behind every happening. Men had to turn away from this to make the scientific discoveries about material causes, but should we not now try to unite both attitudes? Let the rational mind observe scientifically the understandings of the more fertile "unconscious" or superstitious mind and see if they stand the test of time. Balancing the two needs a tight-rope art of continuous adjustment.

It is certainly not suggested we should consult fortune-tellers or practice sympathetic magic to bend the fates to our wishes. There seems to be something wrong about wishing to know the future. And yet on deeper understanding, these are the things that religion is about. One may ask for help in making important decisions and believe the higher religions teach the best ways to "make the invisible powers favourable". But the prosperity or salvation is of the spirit and in eternity rather than in success in this world. "The acceptable sacrifice is a loving and a contrite heart". "Pure religion and undefiled before God and the Father is this, to visit the fatherless and widows in their affliction, and to keep himself unspotted from the world.'' (James 1.27) A minor magic is spring-cleaning, it seems to bring a reward if the time is right.

3. *Theos in History*

That two men with such opposite careers as Stalin and Gurdjieff should have been at the same school in Tiflis together seems an unusually conspicuous sign that there is an Architect, or a team of them, working out plans in the earth's history, and not just mechanical determinism or random chance. ''There is someone behind the curtain'', an Intelligence behind the things that happen. We are not alone, struggling against a meaningless alien universe.

How does genius arise, or a person with such a special fate as Gurdjieff? Genius of varying degree, with the creation of works of art of greater or lesser value, advances in knowledge, inventions – these are the encouraging side of history to counterbalance the so-frequent wars and destructions. The preparation of influential lives is claimed as a kind of evidence of intervention in history by the invisible architects. Genius does not arise in isolation, it is more like a kind of focus for the consciousness and suffering of the times, as Newton saw the apple fall when he was sheltering from the plague, or Jung's ''descent into the Unconscious'' took place while the first world war was raging beyond the frontiers of Switzerland.

One feels that an early death of one member of a family is some times a kind of build-up of potential for another member of the same family. In his chapter Bogachevsky, G speaks of his grief at the death of a favourite sister and how it aroused questions about death and the life beyond the grave. An outside event which may have influenced his development is the Cholera Epidemic of 1892 whose spread is mapped in the Encyclopaedia Britannica – from India across Russia to N. Europe, where sanitary measures kept it under control. G does mention the year 1892; he used the phrase ''discovering America'' to mean something big; possibly this quarter-century of Columbus was a significant year for him (age 14). The Armenian massacres of 1895 and 1896 in neighbouring Turkey must have stirred his feelings.

For this way of thinking: that heaven does rule our affairs, part of the answer to the enigma of Shakespeare's genius – how could a country boy have had such varied and deep experience – lies not in attributing the authorship of the plays to Bacon or some noble Lord, but in the death of Marlowe in a tavern quarrel 30th May, 1593, aged 29, during the plague years of 1592-4, when the theatres were closed most of the time. The connection is pointed by finding they were the same age, both born in 1564, and that though he had become known by his poems, Shakespeare had only just begun to write plays. Superficially the idea is absurd, but as inspiration depends so much on the "Unconscious" with its unknown sources, is it right to deny that this sacrifice may in some way have fused the two careers? Perhaps it did act as a reminding shock, a source of urgency.

Queen Elizabeth I's mother was beheaded before Elizabeth was three; Anne Boleyn's other pregnancies ended in miscarriage and a still-born boy.

G says that after a war some people see the reality of their situation. Dangers and scarcities do show what really matters in life. It seems as if the lives of survivors are not quite their own, they are in debt to those of their generation who were killed. After a night of blitz one felt differently towards the people on the bus, they were no longer strangers, we were all in this together. "Let me survive this and I'll be good for the rest of my life". A girl from the factory was killed in last night's bombing, the place feels different, more real, we are all sharing something.

Perhaps such experiences can be "explained" physiologically, say a release of adrenalin enabling more consciousness, a waking up. It may be that among those who are spared by a general disaster there are some in whom the extra consciousness and urgency can give the creative spark that combines existing material in a new way, such as the next step in understanding gravity. Kepler's life and Koestler's study of the chain Copernicus, Galileo, Kepler, Newton are instructive. Einstein said

"Ideas come from God". Whatever the nature of the processes, one must suppose that the Jews' suffering under Hitler helped the post-war success of Israel, perhaps by giving impetus, arousing sympathy, and compensation for guilt.

What is one to think of another kind of genius, the great adventurers, the Alexanders, Napoleons, Hitlers? Their careers should show up forces that shape history. Such people are often superstitious and are aware of having a special kind of luck, which finally lets them down. Napoleon asked of a prospective commander, "Is he lucky?" His chosen emblem, the bee, seems odd for a war leader; perhaps the sting did have a special meaning for him, which Churchill's cigar also suggests.

Something extraordinary about Alexander of Macedonia is the chain from Socrates through Plato to Aristotle, who was tutor to Alexander, whose conquests prepared the spread of Hellenism. One can see other conquests which did allow the spread of valuable ideas, the Persians under Cyrus, and the Moslems; and even the present dominance of culture of European origin has contributed useful as well as harmful factors; the Empires were not wholly bad. Nationalism in Central Europe got rid of the Austrian Empire only to fall under the empire of Moscow. Different people are in power, nominally they have their own governments, but not much independence, geography is against it. A treasured inheritance from the British Raj is a book of Folk Tales from Tibet collected by Captain W. F. O Connor, Secretary and Interpreter of the mission to Lhassa (1904). It makes one feel Sir Francis Younghusband's armed diplomatic mission to counteract the Russian influence on the Dalai Lama was not too ferocious.

Another influential tutor was Athenodorus of Canana near Tarsus, a Stoic philosopher who taught the young Octavian (Augustus) and followed him to Rome. Among the tutors of the Stoic Emperor Marcus Aurelius Antoninus was a grandson of Plutarch.

The resemblances between Seneca and St. Paul have been attributed to the influence of Athenodorus at Tarsus. The Stoic Lucius Annaeus Seneca was Nero's tutor and was one of the undoubted "martyrs" required by Nero to commit suicide because of jealousy, or for implication in Piso's conspiracy, betrayed by a freed slave named Milichus in A.D. 65, the year after the great fire in Rome. Tacitus describes (thank you Penguin Classics) how Seneca's young second wife Paulina wanted to die with him, but Nero had her wrists bound up and she survived a few years.

Seneca's two brothers (one the Gallio in Acts 18 who would not judge between Paul and the Jews at Corinth) and his nephew the poet Lucan, were among the many other aristocratic Romans who were required to kill themselves. Another was Petronius, Arbiter of Elegance in Nero's pleasures and author of the Satyricon with a famous description of the vulgar luxuries of supper or dinner (cena) with Trimalchio. This name attracts curiosity. "It means thrice blessed and is basically Semitic." But under Porphyry (= purple), biographer and editor of Plotinus, one reads *his* Semitic name was Malchus (= king).

What is the meaning of the leftist anti-church revolutionary chain from Rousseau and Voltaire, the Encyclopaedists, Godwin, Owen, Marx and Engels, Bakunin (father of terrorists and an enemy from whom G may have taken some ideas) to Lenin, Trotsky and Stalin and communism as a new religion? At least the confrontation with communism should make us ask, what *are* the things that matter in human life, and what *do* we know?

Consistency requires the admission that "they" must also have some responsibility in preparing the careers of criminals. How are criminals made? The roots must lie in childhood and before that. One can understand the psychopaths, the not-so-bright, those whose anger quickly becomes violent, perhaps the emotionally twisted, but how is it the cleverer criminals don't see that their activities must eventually lead them into trouble and end in misery? If the police don't catch them, gangsters shoot each other, quite apart from any question of hell in another life. Vanity, out-sized ego seems to be one cause of such blindness. It seems as if the aim of criminology should be repentance and change of attitudes, but how is one to tell if it is genuine?

Defective and emotional thinking, and too-easy systems of ideas which blame all troubles on one enemy, justify much violence. China has used hatred of America; other such enemies are the Reds, the upper classes, the rich, the capitalist system, imperialism, the other race or religion, the Jews, the Germans, the Japs, the armaments manufacturers, the bourgeoisie, or just the majority of society. Hatred is the easy way to unite people into national, class, trade union or other loyalties, which people do need.

Evil, like the poor, will always be with us. It is hard to have a good story without a villain, though the Arabian Nights sometimes manages with only natural disasters like ship wrecks. Some other "villains" are the well-meaning but misguided, unwitting mistakes, tragic fate, and situations that are too complex for any simple right answers.

People who care must try to find the best way of fighting the negative forces and keeping them from getting the upper hand. The obvious means are education, good entertainment, the health services, social work, police and probation, better housing; but these efforts can go wrong and they are being swamped. This is why a rethink of basic ideas and real loyalties seems necessary.

It seems as if God is determined not to be too benevolent, (he "blackens his own face") because we have to develop a kind of independence even of him, by wrestling with evil, first inside ourselves. But when the evil seems overwhelming mercy must be behind it; Lord, have pity, Boss don't make it too hard. "In some ways this work is against Nature and against God." But God fights on both sides. "God is faithful, who will not suffer you to be tempted above what ye are able; but will with the temptation also make a way to escape." (I Corinthians 10.13)

4. Theos and the Occult

There is a whole region of borderline sciences akin to magic and appealing to our natural curiosity and hunger for the miraculous – water-divining, pendulum-swinging, acupuncture, radiesthesia, psycho-kinesis, psychic healing, possibly the Subud latihan, clairvoyance and intentional telepathy; and Kirlian photography which might be of the Theosophists etheric body (the double of the physical body), not the astral. There is the potentisation of homoeopathic remedies by incredible dilutions. Gurdjieff's German chicken soup might refer to Samuel C.F. Hahnemann (1755 – 1843, Hahn = cock), though with all interpretations of Gurdjieff there may be other meanings too. When one is most sure may be just when one has missed some further meaning.

The anthroposophical sciences of Rudolf Steiner, such as sowing seeds by the phases of the moon, are also near to magic. Some of the Steiner sciences remind one of the experiments in the cave of G's Bokharian dervish, though his name Asvatz Truv suggests G's wife Madame Ostrovsky. There was a suggestion that the death of Soloviev in G's *Meetings with Remarkable Men* commemorates Rudolf Steiner (1861 – 30th March 1925). The strange litters in G's Gobi desert story seem to be litres of petrol. The first motorised Central Asian explorations were made 1922 – 1925, using petrol and supplies sent in by camel a season ahead, and found many fossils including dinosaur eggs. At that time it was thought man probably evolved in Asia. One is told Bog is Russian for God; Gobi has Bog spelled backwards.

These sciences seem to operate reliably for some people but are not necessarily repeatable by everyone. Some processes seem to generate emotional energy which is used or transferred locally. One reads that a fire-walking ceremony is prepared by a day of crowd excitement and mounting tension, or of dervishes whose celebration ends by piercing themselves with a knife or a spear, or of poltergeist happenings where there is a disturbed teenager in the house. On the other hand, some telepathy seems to be independent of distance.

The Egyptians said there were two higher bodies, Ba and Ka; perhaps there *is* an intermediate bridging level between the physical and the spiritual. We may be able to learn more about all this in the next world.

One thing which can be said about these borderline ideas is that they show magic may not be all nonsense and so they promote more careful observation. The old and widespread popular beliefs in astrology at least make one realise there may be subtle influences of some sort at work among us, so that one watches for them, and begins to think about individual fate. The symbols of astrology are probably powerful for rousing the "other consciousness". There are also many varieties of fortune telling, the ancient practives of divination such as by the liver of sacrificed sheep or the flight of birds, and the classical belief in oracles. It is sad the last surviving state oracle was ended by the Chinese invasion of Tibet. Not for nothing were the ancient oracles ambiguous. To keep you guessing, hesitating, is typical of the daimons' methods.

The genuine is mixed with showmanship, charlatanism, exploitation of credulity, money-making. The two uses of the word conjuring are instructive. There is probably also a need to protect the genuine against over-exploitation (as with Edgar Cayce) and sensation seekers.

All this borderline region is beyond the competence of the present writer, who can testify that homoeopathic remedies had such potent effects they are now forsworn, but who prefers to attribute all the mysterious powers to direct action by intelligence from another level, rather than to laws which we can manipulate. This view may well be over-simplified.

Perhaps St. Paul has the best answer. "Covet earnestly the best gifts: and yet show I unto you a more excellent way . . . though I have the gift of prophecy and understand all mysteries and all knowledge . . . and have not charity, I am nothing." Self knowledge and the development of conscience is a better way than seeking occult powers, and it may also lead to a sort of magic. But there are rather unmentionable elements in this, to prevent inflation, self-importance.

Georgette Leblanc tells of Gurdjieff saying to her, "I may do it for you". He had powers of concentrating and transferring life forces, but only used them in obedience to the Authority under which he was – if that is a right understanding of him. It would seem that by the transfer of energy on this occasion G enabled Mme Leblanc (Maeterlinck) to surmount her illness, but that it was not a cure for she died a few years later.

* * * * * * *

5. Theos and Us

There are other fancies about subtle unseen connections and transfers of energy. That there is a law of sacrifice seems all too likely.

There is a feeling that unusually beautiful "Battle of Britain" weather is purchased by people dying. Just now, April 1974, we have such a spell which correlates with a tornado in the USA. Logically the idea is absurd, people are dying all the time; but the feeling persists that events play in with the weather, it is part of "the sympathy of all things". It is as if there really were a "Clerk of the Weather" who can regulate it. After all our British weather is so easily varied that foreigners laugh at us for making it a favourite subject of conversation.

Exceptional people have their active years prolonged into the eighties while others are cut off in the 50's and 60's when they should have had more useful years ahead, almost as if their unused possibilities were fed to the others for some special task.

It was observed several times that when someone one knew was dying or had just died, though one may not have known, one felt peculiarly depressed and ill for no real reason. It was as if energy had to be drawn off from the living to help in crossing the river – or was it to remind this body that it too must go some day?

It is not suggested that these fancies actually are direct connections (and certainly not vampirism), just that it is allowed to appear sometimes as if there were such laws to illustrate that "they" do draw off energies to be redirected for other purposes. Suffering is not wasted.

Although there are direct mechanical causes it is felt that accidents are planned by "them". This feeling was strengthened by a run of disasters all of one kind: all to aircraft, charter flights or the three Comet crashes afterwards traced to metal fatigue of the pressurised hulls; or all to ships including the Andrea Doria; or a run of train accidents.

There was a year when all the foxgloves did strange things, every shade between deep pink and white, and the spots also were varied, some quite ferocious like a beast of prey. We learned that an early owner (from 1883 to 1900) of Coombe Springs had been

Sir Charles Douglas Fox, related to the Quaker Foxes. He was a tophatted frock-coated railway engineer who drove daily to his Victoria Street office in his carriage. His grandson, a retired schoolmaster, had called to see the house from which his mother was married, and had given this information. This is an example of the kind of coincidence which fancy calls "a message from the dead surpisingly frequent but usually depending on personal history. The details relate to some one person but it is felt to be given as a collective sign of continued existence.

A recent, unusually elaborate one. Fierce crackling brought out all the neighbours, the pavement was burning furiously, fire engines approached from each side. It was an electric junction box, packed with bitumen, disused since a church was pulled down years before to clear a park for selling second-hand cars. The little boys wanted to become firemen; after the excitement, "Let's go home, we might see it on the telly".

Next summer a fire engine came to lend ladders for a bee-man to take down a swarm settled in a tree just opposite. The same month a fire-engine was in the street again, cooking fat caught fire in a house on the same corner; water pumped into someone's kitchen, not so entertaining.

Fire Brigade three times was too much and started a puzzlement. Then the idea came, F.B., initials used for the Frau Baronin, congenial hostess at the Schloss with the fairy-tale forests, where Hitler's early speeches were heard over the radio, Easter 1933. Far-fetched? Since then, what is this F.B. in an old diary? Why Fish Bowl, the temporary building, a war-time laboratory, where a lot of us lived.

There was a touch of fate about the original connection: the 1931 study sojourn at the Schloss was a last minute arrangement because another hostess in Austria fell ill. An unsuspected link: at a post-war meeting with the Baroness' French friend it was learned the friend had been at Mr Gurdjieff's movements demonstration at the Theatre des Champs-Elysees in 1923. "In the interval he sat at a fountain in the foyer with his arm round several beauties, amidst an oriental decor."

How did this incident get itself recalled and written about? The boy whose mother rang the fire brigade on the third occasion ran across the road in his pyjamas to borrow last year's "calendar" to show the drawing of the fire engine to visitors. They thought the poor little drawing was "fabulous". Reflecting on the undue praise, the connection with fable, the oddity, brought the idea that the story might be a suitable example to tell here.

The "messages" are light-hearted; not so harmless were the many sudden deaths among members of the study groups from about 1954. There were surely too many for the law of averages; they seemed deliberate blows from sinister forces which had us in their grasp, and yet perhaps also implying that a person's death was only an incident, if a serious one, in their on-going life.

Most tragic were the murder of Janet Marshall, a school teacher of 29, on a cycling holiday in France when she went into a wood to relieve herself; and a motor accident which carried off a young mother, also 29, and her mother, leaving father to bring up a year old baby, which he achieved honourably.

At a time when bad news was on its way, one of the warning omens was elderberry jam which boiled over badly, a dark pool of blood on the concrete floor. The "causes" were just the timing of an impulse to use the free fruit, and some inattention, but the sight, still remembered, was a shock. There was also a verbal pun, the victim had been a Subud elder. Is it easier for a man to pour out, lay down his life, because of the nature of his sex? A woman wants to hold on, is more afraid, has to stay behind as a widow, still linked. But one must love life and beauty, and hope to find both again beyond the grave when the time comes.

6. A Bit More Comparative Religion

In "The White Goddess" Robert Graves writes of times when religion changed over from female to male emphasis. One such seems to be Alexandria under the Ptolemies, when Logos was used in preference to Sophia because logos was a masculine word. They must have had good reasons. Too much femininity may produce laxity and abuses; there is a certain cunning in making religion a male prerogative, and one does not know what "unconscious" urges impelled them. But the all-male Trinity is an awkward concept and popular Christianity used the figure of Mary to replace devotion to Isis or the sailors' Queen of Heaven, as Goddess of Mercy, interceding, protecting, helping in trouble. God is a Father who is determined not to spoil his children.

A friend starting Hebrew said the name Mary meant rebellion; denying force, he suggested; recalcitrant idiot? It does not seem to fit very well. Perhaps one may be forgiven for wanting to connect the name with the wrong languages, Mare – sea, or mater.

It is fashionable to laugh at the idea of *hell* or punishment as out-of-date psychology. Why? There are in *this* world so many types of hell: all warfare, trenches, naval gunfire, being torpedoed or bombed, sacking of cities, terrorism, concentration camps, cancer, leprosy, earthquakes, famine – that it does not seem impossible there really are places of punishment or at least severe purgation, in another world. Be that as it may, it has been said the anti-social person really judges himself, shrinking his own being and cutting himself off. "Freedom from fear" is a politicians' promise. Immediate fear may paralyse and is certainly unpleasant, but some contingent fear of future consequences is a necessary stimulus. Stick and carrot are both needed. Our nervous system works by yes-no, stimulus-inhibition, attraction and repulsion, so reward *and* punishment, sensibly balanced, should be the way to train it.

Reincarnation, rebirth into this world, is surely another very ancient human belief. It seems incompatible with the (newer?) Western traditions of "going to heaven", or "eternal life" in some kind of parallel invisible world or worlds. There may be some sense in which it could be reconciled, perhaps as the reuse of the life energies, or of the pattern of fates. The suggestion made here is rather that "reincarnation" takes the form of influencing the minds and lives of the succeeding generations.

The kingdom of heaven is like unto a grain of mustard seed; but a mustard seed is not particularly small, nor does it grow into a tree in which birds can roost. A rather unorthodox explanation is that the hot tasting seed stands for Indian curry, so that the parable would be a way of acknowledging that Buddhism influenced (via the Essenes) the formation of Christianity, contributing the ideas of gentleness and non-violence, and also of monastic self-denial – this explanation is probably all wrong, but it quieted the itch.

A fancy: heaven is not a one-man-one-vote egalitarian democracy. Proportional voting weights itself according to wisdom there. Those who have been faithful in small matters are made rulers over much, but not from any desire to dominate. The masters serve and help to shape the common will.

One feels the gruesome story of Abraham's willingness to sacrifice Isaac must be interpreted symbolically with the 'son' as some other beloved object whose enjoyment may sometimes fruitfully be sacrificed. Like Jacob, Abraham did not submit passively to the Lord but bargained with him that even for ten just men he should spare Sodom and Gomorrah. As there were not even ten, the answer was to remove Abraham's nephew Lot and his daughters from the towns.

Have archaelogists sought the sites of Sodom and Gomorrah? Perhaps they think the search would be in vain, but how the fate of the two cities resembles the destruction of Pompei and Herculaneum in A.D. 79. It seems to be a case of life copying literature.

Plato's Atlantis story, learned from Egyptian priests, is now thought to refer to the destruction of Cretan civilization by the volcanic explosion of the island of Thera or Santorini, followed by huge tidal waves. If Plato's 9000 years are divided by ten the date is about right, 1400 B.C. Like the judgement on Sodom and Gomorrah, Plato interprets the destruction as a judgement on a civilisation which had become corrupt, but one could also interpret it as a sacrifice purchasing the start of Greek culture and so of our civilisation.

At school one heard of the Roman sentry who stood so faithfully on duty at Pompei while the ashes rained down round him, that the excavating archaeologists were able to pour plaster as into a mould and take his model. Somehow it was intimated years back that Gurdjieff's story in the chapter Abram Yelov of the Italian moulder of plaster knick-knacks referred to this. Now it seems that if it points to the similarity Pompei-Sodom it may not be nonsense: Abraham Jehovah – Lover, met when G went to

Tiflis to read ancient literature; G set out to learn the Italian's secrets because his money was "going like the exodus of the Israelites".

7. More Sociology

Sometimes it seems easier to love far-away drought-struck peasants than one's own near neighbours. Loving one's neighbours does not mean loving all the superficial mechanicalness of everyday; the best in me is to love the best in them, but tolerate and manage ordinary manifestations, in them and me, with such skill as is available.

God loving every single one of his children does not mean we should be tender to every violent robber, terrorist, kidnapper, while he persists in his wickedness. The Nazi is not a neighbour until he ***repents***. It has been said even Jesus did not love every one, he did not love the Pharisees. A parallel is Socrates' attack on the Sophists.

Suppose there just are too many people for the earth to support, can one love these multitudes of competitors for basic needs, food, space, a view of the sky? Because it seems "only fair" everyone, who can and wishes, should be "allowed" to replace themselves and their partner, to produce big families in present conditions seems exceptionally anti-social, though it may look right enough on the personal local scale. It is also questionable whether it is right that people with serious inheritable disease should reproduce themselves, as is now becoming more possible.

It is hard to see any adequate answer to the population problem for one cannot wish Nature to reduce our numbers in her own ways, famine, epidemic, tension leading to riot, revolution and war. Maybe she does send earthquakes, droughts and cyclones deliberately, as some have thought.

It seems possible pressure of population in the Roman world had something to do with the early enthusiasm for Christian asceticism. Wrong? the historians complain (repeatedly) of de-population. One can't deny some celibacy would help now, or childless marriages where both partners wish it and find some other creative task together. There is scope for mutual help societies for childless people as they grow older, both single and widow(er)ed. People for whom child-bearing or begetting is contra-indicated could see this as a sacrifice-offering; they can still help with other people's children and so have a share in the next generation. There are cases, such as mental illness, where permitted polygamy might be a better answer than divorce, but it would raise too many legal complications in our society.

The birthrate in the West moves up and down quite easily in response to factors like economic prosperity, unemployment, housing shortage, war-time separations leading to the post-war "bulge", fashionable opinion as to family size, and government policies such as family allowances, so interference should be cautious, but official encouragement of large families seems at least short sighted.

One worries about eugenic aspects, that the big families may be produced by those with poorer heredity; or that immigrants of other races may produce more than their share of the next generation in our already overcrowded country; or that rival religious groups or other minorities try to out-breed each other. All the races have their own talents but that does not say they are not different. Difference should be understood, not concealed; variety makes life richer. Alas, it is often the white skins that look unhealthy. Is not the intellectual often impractical, or bad with people, or artistically insensitive? Still we do need him. Why should not his particular "handicap" be allowed its special schools, which however should also train emotions and body, education for head, heart and hands?

It is sad that even the best-intentioned ***reforms*** do seem to have consequences opposite to the hoped-for benefits. How many of our troubles are due to the reduction of death-rates by medical progress, though one cannot but feel it is right to struggle against disease? Total abolition of the death penalty cannot be unconnected with the increase in violence. Raising compulsorily the minimum school-leaving age, held up as a goal for fifty years, seems to be turning out badly. The successive extensions of the franchise have hardly been introduced for the purest of motives, since the sponsoring party hoped to benefit from the new voters, and the quality of politics has not improved. "No representation without taxation" could be a new slogan, but who is not taxed now?

Regretfully one comes back to Gurdjieff's paradoxical saying, "In order to be a good altruist, you must first be an out-and-out egoist" (see *All and Everything*, p. 1236). Until you know what is really good for yourself, how can you prescribe for others? And in order to give you must first have. Giving in relief of poverty, and provision of basic physical needs after disaster seemed fairly safe, but even this must not be "work to avoid work", to avoid being aware of one's motives and deeper questionings. The same could be said of fasting and various disciplines.

One hopes "Seek ye first the kingdom of God and his righteousness; and all these things shall be added unto you" is a good promise. It does not seem as if superfluities will be provided, but simplicity of living is itself an offering (or prayer).

The only way for society to avoid re-introducing the ultimate sanction of hanging would seem to be by teaching another kind of "death penalty" – the damaging of your own eternal future – and to start teaching it in the junior schools.

Is not a trouble with state socialism, as with huge corporations built by takeovers, simply the inhumanity of size? Do not very large scale organisations have to be bureaucratic and treat people as statistics, and breed a large-scale grumbling? Now we see monopoly on the international scale by the oil-producing countries, and trade unions are monopolies too. Very large schools mean the teachers cannot know all the children's names, let alone their natures.

Here again, with the technological economies of large scale and of standardisation for the mass market, with the demand for more of everything and the need to provide wage employment for increasing numbers, it is hard to see any answer. We cannot go back to a village economy without cataclysm; we do not want the ant-heap of world dictatorship.

What can be said is that no system will work well without good standards of personal conduct, and a better understanding of our own psyche and situation, and so of duties. If these are taught, instead of rights and claims, the mixed system we have would work better. There are no rights against Nature. Is she obliged to provide a living for every mouth that appears? Can one sue her for a disability pension, or God for damages for a fatal accident? Though perhaps in retrospect one may see He did provide survivors with compensation of a sort.

In the debate on contraception and abortion, is there no middle way between restoring the ''baby penalty'', which is punishing the child, and increasing permissiveness, with schoolgirl pregnancies, too-early marriages, and having dates and boy or girl friends being a matter of prestige? Nearly as sad are the many divorces among the legally married, because people are not good to live with and can't see there is something wrong with themselves. The spread of V.D. does suggest Nature is against too much free intimacy. Advertisers and song-writers use sex as the only remaining worth-while goal in life; it is one that cannot be lasting unless there is personal growth; love of ''God'', of an ideal, must be the central striving.

* * * * * * *

So why do baddies, and not so baddies, do bad things? How does the devil get a hold on us and carry out his work of bringing suffering into the world? Vice is vice because it leads to suffering. So is ethics prudence, insurance, not to let the devil get a hold on you? That does not sound very noble! It is felt no real harm can come to you if you are 'trying to live according to the Truth' – or however you express it; but it is not a guarantee of security or prosperity; there will still be suffering, but suffering which buys something.

Yet another list of how troubles come into the world – starting with the moment's inattention when some china gets dropped; ignorance; following the impulse or urge of the moment without realising or caring about the consequences – most seriously in sex, (remembering to use contraceptives is the beginning of responsibility but there are emotional aspects too); belief in one's own cunning, the temptation of easy riches without work, showing off; living in an anti-social milieu where crime against the rest of society, the other religion or race, is admired and justified; all the crimes against one's own health by over-indulgence; the begetting of too many children which is not seen as a crime at all but is one of the surest ways of perpetuating suffering for the parent, the children or society; well-meaning reformers who naturally cannot see far enough.

Apologies are offered for the confusion and repetitiveness of these political platitudes, but one must feel concern over these questions and try to work one's way to better answers, by studying the past for one thing.

Did not Confucius set up the ideal of the good prince, benevolent government? Perfection is unattainable but the existence of the ideal must have an influence even if often used hypocritically for speechifying.

Violent changes only put strong men in power, moderates are swept aside. "Of forms of government let fools contest, whate'er is best administered is best", in the sense of honesty, ability, public spirit. How are these maintained and transmitted to the next generation? By education, art and the media, religion. When these are politically manipulated, what hope is there?

Roman history, remote enough from our own troubles to be viewed dispasstionately, does illustrate this thesis of the importance of standards of personal conduct – the Republic disintegrating into anarchy and rival strong men and tyrannical imperators elected by the military guards. The times of good government were largely due to the influence of the Stoics with their ethical philosophy.

It is true that religion (perhaps from ligare – to bind) has the function of binding society together and supporting established orderly government, but the higher religions with all the human faults of their organisations have kept alive spiritual aspirations.

The symbols and scriptures are preserved to speak afresh to individuals in each new generation and some have ears to hear.

At least a sensible explanation has been met for Pythagoras's injunction not to eat beans, a staple foodstuff. Beans were used for voting, it means avoid politics. The brotherhood did not obey and got disbanded.

In ***Meetings with Remarkable Men*** (p 92) Gurdjieff does speak of "a nationalist movement among the Armenians . . . parties and committees . . . attempts at unity . . . sordid quarrels, in short a violent political explosion . . . with the usual consequences" We can only find the right way with help from "beyond", and "they" will only lead us forward if we pay by our own work and effort towards uprightness. One can only hope being led to write this statement is a step in the right direction.

8. Sex and Family

"If your feet be clean, that is sufficient." What does it mean? One suggestion is that it means clean sex – not so much in adherance to a code of morality, though this is necessary as a general guide, but in respect for the process by which life is continued and in responsible consideration for the other people involved, partner, child, maybe also partner's legal spouse.

Thou shalt not beget an unwanted child.

Faithfulness is the chastity of marriage.

Humans mate face to face, they are meant to meet as whole people, not just as quadrupeds from behind. We become capable of physical sex before we are full-grown, but does not the too early pursuit of it interrupt development? Men and women have a great deal to give each other that is not just physical sex.

Naturally,the male, whose reproductive function is easily aroused and quickly performed, tends to like a more permissive polygamous or promiscuous morality than the female who has the long-lasting responsibility of pregnancy and rearing. Human marriage tries to tie the father down to helping in this responsibility with the inducements of domestic comforts and an heir, but surely many older men would testify that fatherhood brought them fulfilment. Children educate their parents as well as the other way round. One feels it is not wrong to ask the security of monogamy, and physical faithfulness as a sign of it, but this does not mean exclusive possessiveness. "Love of consciousness evokes the same in response, Love of feeling evokes the opposite, Love of body depends only on polarity and type." (*A & E* p 361.)

"In the resurrection they neither marry, nor are given in

marriage, but are as the angels of God in heaven'' – if we knew what that was – wider union? (Matt. 22.30)

Someone joined the Australian forces in the war of 1939-45 to get away from home and a possessive managing sort of mother. When she died not long after the war, he felt remorse, for one does owe a lot to one's mother. We cannot force ourselves to love, but forgiving one's parents for their mistakes – which they could blame on their parents and so on back to original sin – must be a way of freeing oneself from the consequent emotional habits.

Sex leads into magic and it is a pity to spoil it.

Love that refrains, restrains itself when the time is not ripe, is self-transcendent.

Creation comes through weakness; weakness of the mother, strength of the father; but a man is the mother of his own soul.

The stirring up of emotions by love affairs seems to stimulate the creative process for poets and artists, but the torments are not enviable.

The ideal for a human being may be to unite male qualities of courage and adventure with female qualities of artistic sensitivity and warmth, (or whatever is on your favourite lists). The division into active and passive, male and female, and other dualisms would seem to be very fundamental; sex has been a great teacher and played a part in all religions, but the most precious and the worst are here very close together.

9. *Guidance and Payment*

The anti-sex monastic trend in Christianity may have been a necessary corrective to excesses the other way, such as temple prostitution, and yet both have been intended to elicit an imaginary psychic kind of sex, Christ the bridegroom of the soul. Such experiences are a sort of evidence of non-physical reality which is also liable to intrude in an immediate and bodily way by unpleasant sensations that convey no, stop, wake up, do something different – though not in words.

There would seem also to be positive kinds of guidance; a

picture of doing some job, perhaps with a method not thought of before, presents itself repeatedly in the head; or the idea of an action having arisen by combination of various circumstances, one feels persistently impelled to do it though one would rather not. Reactions or remarks that came out quite unconsciously may seem on looking back, to have been guided, for instance if they resolved a hesitation about what to do. You realise "Well, it's no good worrying, it's 'their' business, if 'they' want it, 'they'll' see to it", and presently you find the answer comes of itself. If the hint comes through the cat wanting attention or a small child arriving, it seems safe that it was not just your own will. If there are no interruptions it is all right to go ahead as planned.

The Quakers have experience of testing their "concerns" to see if they are genuine. But even when you do have to follow the guidance it may be leading you up the garden, or by a round-about route. George Fox in his Journal, mentions a man who "had run out into imaginations", or a woman who was cured and "ran to words" and had to be warned to keep low. Two quotations from Fox are worth copying; one feels they might apply to George Gurdjieff too. "Our Labour is to bring all men to their own Teacher in themselves." "The Lord had given me a spirit of discerning, by which I many times saw the states and conditions of people, and could try their spirits."

It is considered "*they*" are at work everywhere, but perhaps more concentratedly at significant points in a lifetime – birth, copulation and death – or places in society, and that the more definite guidance must be in connection with some purpose of theirs, not our wishes. There also seems to have to be payment, or tax, or sheepshearing; one can't say exactly why it is necessary, perhaps a combination of reasons woven together, since "they" seem to like "killing several birds with one stone".

At first sight the story in Beelzebub's "First Descent" has an odd subject, the young do-gooder who thought he could help people by letting them off paying taxes. Then one recalls that Luke also starts with a tax-story: "And all went to be taxed, everyone into his own city", and realises that the heavenly

Government, like earthly ones, does exact taxes. We hope the taxes are used for purposes benevolent to us, but whether the Government has other needs we cannot tell.

The payments exacted can be poor sleep, a kind of "enclosure", rather phoney aches and pains; these perhaps are used where a passive kind of "work" is wanted. "For every satisfaction you must pay", one way or another, partings, destructions, breakages, rebuffs (raspberries, arrows, stonings) – till one almost fears to enjoy the satisfactions, unless one can hope they have been paid for in advance; but at least one can feel of the dissatisfactions, they must be *for* something, compensation will come.

Perhaps one may say Mr. G's first motor accident was his payment for writing ***Beelzebub***, or part of it. Exile, financial problems Mme Ostrovsky's illness – there cannot have been any lack of struggles, and all the time big responsibilities. Miss Merston said that the first chapters of ***Beelzebub***, from number two, were dictated when he was almost unconscious after the accident. Afterwards he had no memory of that time. He gave it all as "I hear, I am told". Only after that period did he write from himself.

She told how he got up about a week after the accident, still half conscious, and had bonfires lit in various parts of the estate, watching each burn. He taught some new movements, then stopped again. Some time later he said he could never have taught those, much too difficult; so they showed him, and started having classes again at night for the 30-40 people living at the Prieuré. The "science of idiotism" – the toasts, originated about this time. (Stanley Nott, ***Teachings of Gurdjieff: The Journal of a Pupil***).

10. *At the Flat*

Mr. Gurdjieff's Russian habit of late suppers, by putting visitors to his Paris flat out of their daily clock rhythm, was one factor in breaking through the surface shell and exposing the essence. As one walked down the short Rue des Colonels Renard and climbed the stairs to the first floor, meeting the smell of spices, one seemed able to switch over to a more attentive state; this was a vital moment in one's lifetime that could not come often, but bewildering too, disturbing comfortable accepted notions. G did not fit the conventional picture of a saint, with his lavish food in a still-rationed world, the vodka and the armagnac: he could be called "glutton and wine-bibber", though one did not see the model then.

Before the meal we sat uncomfortably crowded on the floor or on high backless stools, trying to keep attention on the reading. During that year 1948-9 we began to have duplicated chapters of ***Beelzebub*** on loan but the enjoyable Second Series was available only at these readings. G would come in and sit in his worn fauteuil, smoking through a holder. The atmosphere lightened. He would laugh happily at his own old jokes, insist on an absurd pronounciation, or that a word be changed. Lisa would put her head in the door to count how many couverts were needed.

One tried not to look at his poor dropsical stomach with the trousers falling down. On our first visit he wore no shirt, only a vest as in the photo; one felt that it was to test the straightlaced English, but it was more than that. At Easter he wore a beautiful Russian shirt, white with cross-stitch on the collar, and there was pascha, a rich preparation of cream cheese, eggs, raisins, crystallised fruit, with kulitch, a sweetened bread.

During the long meal one had to stay awake, in spite of heaviness from the heat and the alcohol, and keeping track of emptying one's glass in 3 toasts (men) or 6 (women), in case G should say something significant. "Here no one ever drunk"; the salad was "medicine", full of oil. (No one ever saw Socrates drunk).

At the three small dining tables pushed together, Mr. G sat on a small upright sofa (sophia?) with the Director for toasts on his left, and poubelle, égout, bonche d'égout squeezed in to right and left. To this dustbin and drain would be handed food and drink he could not finish. A horror was a sheep's head cooked whole; choice bits were passed to favoured people. Sometimes the favour was half a croissant dipped in sour cream; then one longed to be the favoured one, that feeling must be put aside.

A "very special compote from Morocco" (?) seemed to be ordinary English marmalade; some shredded "cheese" tasted of soap; small peppercorns, "very hot, eat bread with them", tasted quite mild. Some sheep's cheese was offered; thinking it was to torment instinctive centre, the mouth was opened wide to swallow it. "Give, give" he said. Most ashamed, the recipient hastily cut it into small portions, no time to count how many, and handed them round.

There seemed very little that was new, just the standard stories, gifts of food to individuals, the toasts to the idiots, but the smallest things grew full of meaning later. His remarks were eagerly reconstructed at Café discussions next day. We heard that he once added "If doubting idiot will work honourable, I will drink with him all night". That was encouraging to people who feared they were doubting idiots.

"To all zig-zag idiots, who have five Fridays a week". Friday only suggested pay-day, it seemed meaningless. It was years before one connected it with Good Friday.

"The English are very stupid. Three Englishmen climbed a hill to look at the view. After twenty minutes the first said, 'I think today will rain'. After twenty minutes more the second said, 'I think today not will rain'. After another twenty minutes the third said, 'I not like so much conversation', and they all went home again."

"The Irish are very dirty. An Irishman and his son were journeying when they came to a river and sat down to take off their boots and socks before wading across. 'Father', the son said, 'your feet are much dirtier than mine'. 'But son, I've been in the world twenty years longer than you'."

"Scotch are very stingy. Scot wanted to commit suicide. He turn on gaz and put his head in oven. Then he began to mentate. Man never stops mentating so long he live. He think 'How many shillings costet gaz?' Then he decide not to kill himself today, and he turn off the gaz." Russian, like Latin and early Greek, does not have the definite and indefinite articles – 'the' and 'a'.

"On right shoulder Angel, on left shoulder Devil", he told one young woman; to which did she listen?

Mr. G was fond of philologizing, as in ***The Arousing of Thought***, where he complains that English has the same name for the highest and for the lowest and dirtiest thing in man, soul and sole of the foot.

There was a very involved story about a chateau where he first learned the toasts of the idiots. He needed very badly to go to the water closet, at last the priest beside him had to half-carry him like a child. The priest, he roar with laughter, "next time, you tell". It is suggested that the chateau was St. John's gospel with its symbolism of the true Vine and its 21 Chapters and the water into wine miracle of the marriage at Cana, and that Father Giovanni in the Chapter ***"Professor Skridlov"*** represents the evangelist.

The high number idiots were seldom reached, but one heard that God himself was the highest number, 21, and Mr. G was number 18. They were grouped in threes. Number one, Ordinary idiot, then Super and Arch; then the first series of geometric idiots, Round idiot all round, Square – not idiot at the corners, and Zig-zag; then Compassionate, who was only compassionate "when fiancée look out of window"; Hopeless, and Recalcitrant, who had to be threatened with the carving knife. Later ones included Doubting, Borning, and Fanfaron or Boasting; and Illuminated who knew what to do but could not do it.

After some visits you were to choose which idiot you thought you were, and the Director, when he called a toast, was to remember and name those present who had chosen that idiot. Progress could be up: "Round, cadidate for Square", or confusingly, down towards number one and then up again.

Rather special was "To all Hopeless idiots, subjectively and objectively, that is to those who will die an honourable death and to those who will early lately perish like dog, like dirty dog," with its "addition", "only those will die an honourable death who have worked on themselves during life".

An obscure story was about a chateau he wanted for the future of the work – up a big stairway to a hall for movements, then up more steps to a home for the author of ***Beelzebub.*** Later it was seen to be a garbled description of the house in Colet Gardens, formerly Henry Moore's studio and now the Royal Ballet School, which the Ouspensky groups acquired for meetings shortly before the war and which was to be a joint centre for all the London groups. It has an extraordinary and wide staircase running straight up the whole centre of the building, but the big hall was at the top and the living quarters led off the half landing. A glass conservatory was unsafe and had to be pulled down.

At the flat we laughed once when Alfred Etievant-Estival tried to speak English. "I need his English" Mr. G said. We understood why when Alfred came to be our movements teacher in London. He has since died prematurely, (in 1968?). "Diacre" – deacon (diakonos = servant, minister) Mr. G called him, and he looked it with his dark hair and angular serious face.

When did Mr. G say something like this? Everything is relative and depends on situation. Even turning the other cheek is not right always, but in the right situation "one man will learn a lesson he will not forget in a thousand years". Does a man exist for a thousand years? That is cheering.

We new visitors did not know that dropsy was the reason for Mr. Gurdjieff's swollen pregnant abdomen, but when he finally went into the American hospital in Paris, we heard that twelve litres of fluid were withdrawn. It seemed a last joke, litters.

It was as if he consented to go into hospital because he felt it was time for him to die. The publication of *All and Everything* had been put in hand. He slipped away in a coma after a week. We were told the doctor was convinced G was conscious, against the normal rules. Rest in peace, but one feels such a man after a short holiday would be working again, to carry out what had been prepared.

* * * * * * *

III
LANGUAGES OF THE OTHER CONSCIOUSNESS

1. *Spelling*

By now it may be apparent that though the fable is fiction, it is an attempt to express experiences through the "Unconscious" in the shelter of the Coombe Springs Community. Their validity must be judged by whether their fruits are useful.

The Unconscious is a thoroughly confusing subject. We owe a debt to Freud and the others who have made this neutral term respectable in rationalistic conversation, so that all sorts of unexplained things can be lumped together in it without prejudging whether they are natural or supernatural, demonic or Holy Ghost. But we still do not know what it is. Unconscious does not seem a good translation of ***unbewusst***; it is outside our personal consciousness but might be more conscious than we are. However one cannot fix on a better word. Mme de Hartmann prefers to translate the title of Eduard von Hartmann's book "Philosophy of the ***Unknown***".

One of its characteristics is Power – things happen; another is Fertility, it produces lots of ideas, images, connections, but they do need vetting by the conscious, critical mind. F.W.H. Myers, son of Frederick Myers, used the term subliminal, below the threshold. "The subliminal mind is gold mine as well as a rubbish dump", but the rubbish does need a lot of sifting.

In ***Beelzebub's Tales***, Gurdjieff seems to prefer the word subconscious, and the analogy of belowness, depth, is good, but some people use subconscious for an intermediate level between conscious and unconscious, i.e. all the latent memories which can be recalled by the right triggers. These are one's own stock-in-trade of mental furniture, experiences, information, basic ideas. It is an argument for collecting good ''furniture'' – strong, useful, beautiful, maybe some genuine antiques – so let gratitude be recorded for having been made in childhood to listen to Bible readings, and learn a few passages by heart from the Sermon on the Mount, or from Paul's epistles; and for meeting later with all Gurdjieff's seminal ideas.

One of the first things this person's unconscious did when it got activated was to start developing a queer system of spelling, probably arising from Gurdjieff's made-up words. All the words having the same consonants, in any order, are reckoned to have some connection. Some groups were energised by the names of gods, starting with ***STR*** from Astarte, Easter, rest, interest, star, stair, tears, uterus, U(l)ster, Tarsus, (it means heel); and seven, Cevennes, Venice, Viennese, finance, Zenith from Venus. ***H*** does not count. Eventually the consonants were reduced to nine:

K, G & C(hard)	) Mnemonic for this group Egypt		
T, D	) (hard G) or Cupid		
P, B	)		
S, soft C	(which can be stretched to	)	
R	include Sh, Ch, Z, soft G, J)	)	Mnemonic
L		)	Israel
F, V, Th, Ph	) Mnemonic Phenomenon,		
N	) St. Venoma, Venom		
M	)		

Some favourite groups are:

Refaim (weak ones, the dead – Phoenician and Hebrew)
– farm, frame, pharmacy, Ephraim, form, Murphy, Arimathea

Thelema (will) – fulm, flame, thalamus

Ophis (snake) – sophia, office, fish, Joseph

Calvary – cavalry, cavalier, calf, clever, clover, Glover, Valkyrie, California, Virgil, gravel

Devil – Teufel, left, felt, fault. (The group evil, live, devil, deliver was an introductory lesson.)

Satan – Saint, Sutton, stain, stone, Stanley, Sydney

Seraph – first, freeze, suffer, Pharisee, Orpheus

Grave – graph, vigour, growth, curve, Vigurs

Cavern – Katherine, govern, Frank, Veronica, caravan, Corinthian, Craven, African, carving, fir-cone

Garden – Gordon, Gadarene, grand, Din-gir – a god (Sumerian), tarragon, Tengri, carton, Croton (where Pythagoras taught)

Mother – thermos, thermodynamics

Demon – daimon, demonstration, dynamics, demand, mend, mind, Mendham, mint, anatomy

Stephanos (it means crown) – invest, phantasy, thanatos (death), footnotes, fasting, defence, deafness, unbewusst, stiffen, Tiffen's school, inventiveness, sensitive, St. Swithin, negativeness, Ctesiphon, (ma)nifesto, Da Vinci

Natal – Donald, London, dandelion, talent, Italian, Atlantis, handle, Daniel

Mark – Karl Marx, Bismarck, Marx brothers (clowns), Makarios (blessed), Kramer, Marduk, market, Mercury, Marconi, Masaryk

Logos – Lagash, Lagos, galosh, school, class, Aeschylus, Ezekiel

Pluto – Plato, plate, plateau, Pilate, Plotinus, depilate, plot, pilot

Verb (the Word) – fibre, brief (which is letter in German, Farbe – colour.)

Christ (Anointed) – security, electricity, skirt, strike, crystals, stroke, Etruscan, (J.L.) Starkey, Turkestan, turquoise, criticism, secateurs, streak, Socrates, cortex, crust, aristocrat, scratch,

Phallus – false, philosophy, slave, Slav, self, Flavius, syphilis

Nature – Neter (Egyptian), train, Taranis, but also andros (man), Andrew, Indra.

Damascus – Semitic, mystic, cosmetic, mosquito, mask, mosque, Max, Moscow, cosmos

Friend – defender, fender, fortune, front, Ferdinand, Nefertiti

Scarab – practice, Carabas, scrappy, scrape, Abraxas; or any three of the four sounds: scar, crab, pax, stick

Sacrifice – scarf, scurf

Paris – purusha, purse, brush, price, Persia, Broussa, Bruce, Basra, Berossus

Nile – kneel, Neil, lean, nylon, Lenin, line, senile, Lyne, li

Sumeria – Samaria, summer, Somerset, somewhere, Morris, Rams

Nazareth – Firenze (Florence), Zirvan, Zeravshan (river)

Polis (town) – police, supplies, supplice (torture)

Angel (Messenger) – angle, glen, ankle, uncle, clean

Archetypal – Plutarch

Aphrodite – Ford, Freud (Freude = joy), draught, fraud

Heracles (= Glory of Hera) – Carolus, Lewis Carroll, Eresh-Kigal

Simon – semen, shaman, menses, insomnia, snow-man

Penis – pension, expense, spin, Spain, pence

Skin – foreskin, Nusku, Jenkins, Jackson, Shekinah

Porne (harlot) – born, brain, burn, Bryn, Nippur, prune, pioneer brown, robin, barn, bairn

Georg (George – husbandman) – organ

Ahriman – harmony, Armenia, Roman, Norman

Abraham – Brahma, Hammurabi, "Brm, Brm" (children's motor car noise)

Pleurs (tears) – labour, Beryl, pearl, parler (to speak), leper

It is not quite such an earth-shattering magic secret as one felt at first, but it was a training in flexibility, setting up new connections, and useful for taking hold of a new name or foreign word. Some languages, like Arabic and old Egyptian, do use triliteral roots; and authors may put special meanings into the proper names they give their characters.

Since this was drafted, the S. volume of the encyclopaedia belatedly revealed that Pitman's shorthand is based on a rather similar phonetic simplification. Later still something was found in "The Definitions of Asclepius unto King Ammon" – "Thrice Greatest Hermes", G. R. S. Mead, Vol. II, p 170:

"For that its very quality of sound, the very power of Egyptian names, have in themselves the bringing into act of what is said.

"As far as, then, thou canst, O King – (and thou canst do all things) – keep this our sermon from translation; in order that such mighty mysteries may not come to the Greeks, and the disdainful speech of Greece, with all its looseness, and its surface beauty, so to speak, take all the strength out of the solemn and the strong – the energetic speech of Names.

"The Greeks, O King, have novel words, energic of argumentation only; and thus is the philosophising of the Greeks – the noise of words." (But it is in Greek that it has been preserved for us).

Is not this one reason the King James Bible keeps its power? The old translators, including the martyred William Tyndale (c 1492 – 1536), understood the magic of words and tried to choose equivalents with similar sounds, or their own richness of association.

Philosophy may lose its real point in translation, if it is built around key words with double meaning.

"In the beginning was the Word". Language, the great achievement of humans, can also be their enemy. This Egyptian feeling for words of power may preserve some taste of one way in which language originally developed – one of the mysteries of prehistory.

* * * * * * *

2. *Gurdjieff's Words*

An ambulance went by. As we live near the hospital we often hear an ambulance siren. ***Siren, nurse,*** (Nature is the old nurse), ***ouranos*** (heaven, sky). G's word, the sacred ***Rascooarno*** – death – came to be ***sarc–ourano*** (flesh as in sarcophagus) – Heavenly flesh, resurrection body.

Some of Gurdjieff's made-up words seem capable of many interpretations; so long as they make sense they may all be useful. These are some personal ones:

Triamazikamno – Tree (the Cross) a magic name
Tree love sick man

Heptaparaparshinokh – He Pta (father) prepare part, He knock (sends trouble)

Hanbledzoin – Johan B (John the Baptist) led Zion

Zerlikner (doctor) – Like Nerzer, like the Nazarene

Parktdolgduty – Practice Gold Duty – the golden rule.
Confucius' negative form was "What you do not like when done to yourself, do not do to others". Another form is in Kingsley's ***Water-Babies,*** the fairy Doasyouwouldbedoneby with her less pleasant sister MrsBedonebyasyoudid.

For Ashiata Shiemash, one came upon the echo: Ishtar Shamash (Sin) the Babylonian triad for Venus, Sun (Moon); or again She a Mashiah Ta, the earth thankful for Messiah.

Polormedekhtic – parlour maid – Gladys Aylward the missionary. Mary of Bethany. The name Toof-Nef-Tef for the king of the planet Mars, ***A & E p 1147,*** was held to echo an Egyptian name like Pharaoh Tuthmosis III, the conqueror, 1484 – 1451 BC, with his possible connection with Moses.

The narrow swinging bridge over the Pyandzh river, or over the Zeravshan on which Bokhara stands, ***R.M.*** p 149: finding that piangere is the Italian for "to weep" it seemed the Pyandzh might be the river of tears – human suffering.

Pirmarals – *A & E* p 208. Atlanteans hunting for them settled by the Sea of Beneficence. The Pilgrim Fathers went to America in search of "pure morals". On the other hand, Grafton Elliot Smith in ***"The Evolution of the Dragon"*** 1919 and his disciple W. J. Parry in ***"The Children of the Sun"*** thought all early culture, particularly the megalithic, came from Egypt, carried mainly by sea by small groups seeking an elixir of life. G's Atlanteans founded ***Maral-pleicie,*** moral play see, even Molière play see? Turn m r l round for lemures, spirits of the dead, whence lemur "kinds of nocturnal mammal specially of Madagascar, allied to monkeys". The ancient Romans held May was an unlucky month for marriages because of the Lemuria, the festival of the unhappy dead.

Belcultassi – *A & E* p 249, who worked to be able to be quite sincere with himself, and founded the society ***Akhaldan*** on Atlantis: one could read it Bel, cult Lord of Assyrians or Akkadians, particularly as one is inclined to connect Akhaldan with Chaldaean, a rather elusive term. There are also Khaldians, early inhabitants of Armenia or Urartu (Ararat), from their chief god Khaldi. However Belcultassi was made into a complicated anagram: Bull tass ice, Bull as an old symbol for God, tasse for cup, fate: God's cup the Ice Ages. A quaint formula was found "He sculpt the earth and she sculpt us". God or cosmic forces do things to continents and climates which affect the evolution of life. The large scale "creative suffering" of the Pleistocene (plasticine) Ice Ages, forced the evolution of homo sapiens and the developed stone age hunting cultures (of which a few last survivors have reached our own times, valuing courage, and allowing us to get some taste of what life was like for our long-ago ancestors).

In the chapter "Why 'Men' and not Men" we read that the High Commission of Angels and Archangels, with the help of the Arch-Chemist-Physicist Angel Looisos, caused the organ Kundabuffer to grow at the base of the spinal column of the three-brained beings breeding on the ill-fated planet Earth. This

Looisos was held to be Louis Agassiz, 1807 – 1873, Swiss, of Huguenot extraction. He studied living fish, then fossil fish, then other fossils. In 1836 he started to study the Swiss glaciers. Certain geological deposits, clays and gravels, associated with scratched blocks of stone foreign to the locality, had been attributed to Noah's Flood and called Diluvium. Agassiz soon came round to the views of some earlier workers that these deposits were due to glaciation and that great sheets of ice, like those remaining in Greenland, once covered all the countries in which unstratified gravel, (boulder drift) is found. An English geologist, Buckland, who had published a book called ***Reliquiae Diluvianae,*** invited him on a joint tour of Britain and was converted by Agassiz' observations to the Ice Age explanation.

In 1848 Agassiz became Professor of Zoology at Harvard. He was evidently one of the nineteenth century's beloved professors, like Pasteur, whose last words to his students were "il faut travailler" and William James (1842 – 1910) who went on Agassiz's expedition to the Amazon in 1865, but came back ill. "If you study nature in books, when you go out-of-doors you cannot find her" said Agassiz. He was unsympathetic to Darwinism, partly because to him each species of animal or plant was in itself "a thought of God". He had an intensely religious mind, though he was out of sympathy with sects or creeds. At his burial, the students sang a requiem. One wrote, "He had been a student all his life long, and when he died he was younger then any of them".

Old Merv, Old Weimar, Moravians, Ave Maria. Did G intend the association with Weimar (German W = our V), which with the neighbouring university of Jena (both now, alas cut off from us in E. Germany), was such a *marv*ellous centre in non-unified Germany in Goethe's time?

The Moravian brethen, a strikingly unquarrelsome church, date back to followers of John Huss and to the Waldenses. They were nearly extinguished by the Protestant defeat in 1620, but their bishop Comenius kept together a remnant as a "hidden seed". At fresh persecution, they fled to Germany where Count Zinzendorf (1700 – 1760), a Pietist, let them build a settlement,

Herrnhut, on his estate. He organised them into a "militia Christi" based not on monasticism but on the family.

John Wesley was on the same ship with a party of Moravians emigrating to Georgia in 1735, and saw during a storm that their faith was more real than his. After further contact Wesley had his "conversion" in 1738 during a reading from Luther at a meeting. Goethe was influenced by the Moravians and by a Pietist friend of his mother's, when he turned to alchemy and mysticism during the long illness which stopped his studies in Leipzig. A period of illness leading to fruitful reflection is found in other biographies; William James is another.

Schleiermacher (1768 – 1834) theologian and philosopher, was educated at a Moravian school and seminary. As his name means veil-maker one may be allowed to associate from G's "after dinner Cheshma" of Sheherazade, with footnote "Cheshma means veil", *A & E* p 10, to all the other confusing German Sch's around 1800, Schiller, Schelling, Schopenhauer, the Schlegel brothers who began Sanskrit scholarship in Germany.

"Novalis", the romantic poet, born 1772, whose death from consumption in March 1801 is like an inaugural sacrifice for the new century, had grown up in the atmosphere of the Herrnhuter; he was enthusiastic about Friedrich Schlegel's early project to found or announce a new religion, and wrote hymns for it.

All this is material for the question of *affiliation*. Though real vivification must come from within and in some cases may seem to arise quite independently, in others personal contact plays a part. There are families with several distinguished members, or the chains from master to pupil among the philosophers or the physicists, or the circle around a person like St. Teresa of Avila, the Platonic Academy at Florence, the early members of the Royal Society in London, or the Romantic schools at Jena and Heidelberg.

The Pietists and Moravians concerned themselves with missions to Red Indians and Eskimos, and with schools, an important work. One wishes that everyone could remember from their youth some older people or teachers whom they respected and wanted to become like, or who communicated an enthusiasm.

3. *Puns and Symbols*

Another language is of puns connected with the names of things, so that everyday happenings can start associations:

Helicopter – He like opfer (sacrifice)
Tea – sacrifice (from the Tau cross)
Tray – traitor, tea-tray – Judas
Tea and beer – for less mentionable fluids or pseudo-fluids. Beer is a well in the Old Testament.
Cocoa – co, with, together, intercourse
Ironing – irony
Crocuses – crosses, small ones
Glove, clothes-horse – Golgotha
Shoe – Yeshua
Bus – subconsciousness
Cup – fate
Artichokes – arty jokes (which the dog Philos brought to G. *R.M.* p 139)
Ginger – G. I. Gurdjieff, who gingered people up (also surgeon is for him by its inner rhyme)
Bubble – Beelzebub
Herbs – Herbert
Hyphen, trait d'union –penis, (also trade union)
Cough – coffin, Box – coffin, Coffee – coffin
Grease – Greece
Sciatica – sigh - Attica (Greece)
Natural dye, colour – die
Legs – legacy (leave something useful behind)
Potatoes – potestas, power
Dog – God
Liver – book (livre) (compare le foie –liver, la foi – faith)
Gland, glandiness (stiff neck) – England
Juice – jews
Plums – Olympus (spells symbol)

Ties to wear – ties, relationships

Snow, sun – son

Knot – Thou shalt not

Socks – sex

Toast to eat – toasts, drinking healths

Mess – message

Moustache – Messiah, task

Dates to eat – dates in history, chiefly two, of birth and death

Creamline on milk – Kremlin (other spellings, gremlins, lacrima – tear)

Salad – is like a word for prayer, salat, in Arabic

Aphis, aphides – is a fides, taken to mean people without faith, garden pests

Leeks (vegetable) – leaks through the roof, supposedly also "leaks from outside" into one's head

Knitting (& weaving) – "tinking" (thinking)

Making lists – the wind that bloweth where it listeth (not to mention flatulence). The text about people born of the spirit being like the wind (John 3.8) was held to have suggested G's story about the difference between stringed and wind musical instruments in the favourite chapter ***"The Bokharian Dervish"*** (*A & E* p 881)

Moth – mother

Fat – fate

Temples (side of forehead) – con–templation (con – with)

Marmalade – ma malade (mother ill)

Rhubarb – Barbara

Shelf – self

Lace – soul

Raspberries, gooseberries – rebuffs (sharp taste)

Eiderdown – ideas

Shoulder – soldier

Screwdriver – Gurdjieff

Lorry driver	– Lord(s) river?
Candle	– Alexandria (for the Pharos lighthouse). Scandal, sandal, sandalwood, brought Alexandria by sound.

There is some joke about Boots, coinciding with the fashion for long boots to keep mini-skirted legs warm, (mini– ministering, which St. Mark was useful for) that has never been properly understood. Is it for Caligula, kickname from caligae, army boots; or for Paul's missionary journeys on foot, or for life in general, keep plodding down the road? (But when the feeling comes, "plod on somehow" it is often a sign to do the opposite, stop, and bring up wind which is all that is ever found in this particular solar plexus now-a-days). Or is it for Italy shaped as a high-heeled boot, Roman dominance?

Bicycle still carries a feeling charge though one can no longer be sure what the meaning was – dual psyche, two people working together; or conscious and unconscious?

Check (coat)	– cheque (book)
Bucket	– for kicking – dying
Pub, public house	– pubic
Varicose veins	– very close Venus
Spaghetti	– Spettigue, (spells Egypt, perhaps also Peskett, the undertaker's assistant)
Champagne	– sham pain
Fringe	– Thring
Rope	– Europe
Continent	– land area, and the self-controlled
Rag	– ragazzo (boy)
Jam-making	– traffic jams on Bank Holiday
Berry	– bury
Fruit	– result
Thunder	– fun at the door
Peach	– péché, sin; pécher, to fish
To know	– used with sexual meaning in the Bible
Trolley	– Lord

Geometry – geo-mater, Mother Earth, (mater – matter, material)

Smith – myth, Memphis, city of the artisan god Ptah, capital of the Old Kingdom of Egypt and of the pyramids

Oats – Tao

Onion – union

Almond – All the world (monde)

Deer – dear

Genital – gentle; the strong should be gentle, fathers not bullies

Dick – dikaiosynis, righteousness

Tarpaulin had an intriguing sound but what should it mean? – St. Paul, trap all in?

Kidney – child born (nee)

Rash (skin trouble) – Russian, ration. Why not self-rationing of alcohol, tobacco, food to keep yourself the right weight? However, some are rationed by indigestion so can't preach. About smoking, Kathryn Hulme tells in ***"Undiscovered Country"*** (p 105) how after a year's total abstaining, G tricked her into smoking one of his Russian cigarettes and so set her to follow "the harder path, the golden middle way between abstinence and excess".

Kettle was supposed to mean balance, the golden mean, middle way, balanced judgement, from Mene, mene, tekel, upharsin (Daniel 5.27), weighed in the balance and found wanting. Other spellings: Celt (much more convincing with K, Keltic) kilt, cult, quality, Tikliamish. No clear meanings have been found for G's Tikliamishian civilisation but there is a Takla Makan desert. Perhaps the rules are a bit too elastic for they could add Chaldea.

Plant names suggest quite a number. Forget-me-not and Honesty need no translating.

Onagraceae – (evening primrose, willowherb) – grace

Cruciferae – (four petalled, mustard, wall-flower) – cross

Buddleia – (from Buddle, a botanist) – Buddha

Fuchsia	– (from Fuchs, 16th century German botanist) – Confucius
Willow, willowherb	– God's will
Cyclamen	– cycle of menstruation
Cherry	– the sadness of Chekhov's cherry orchard cut down
Dahlias	– daily ah's, sighs
Phlox	– Philo Volume X
Leaf	– belief, also bay-leaf for seasoning, and Glauber's salts Kder Glaube – faith) stands for belief
Grass	– grace
Sage (herb)	– sage, wise man
Thyme	– time
Mint	– mind
Geranium	– ger, client, lover
Dock	– doctor (& Gurdjieff)
Hydrangea	– high danger, danger of heights
Iris, rose	– Eros. Roses also neuroses and "rose from the dead"
Wire	– why-er, one who asks why? The Wye and Wylye rivers ask why,my uncle's Wylye river down which Stonehenge stones were brought

Greedy puss – to rhyme with Oedipus. Not that the Oedipus complex ever conveyed much, but one has read that Sophocles' Oedipus at Colonus is a prototype of the suffering saviour, who pays more than his own share.

Elastic – eschatology, from eschatos – last, about the End of the World and the Day of Judgement, an unscientific expectation; but scatology is the study of coprolites, fossil dung, both skor, skatos and kopros being Greek for dung.

Sore eyes – G's Aïsors – sore "I", the discomfort of being displeased with yourself.

Pole, Polish seems to mean something more than the country Poland: polis – town or police? more probably the opposite pole in magnetism and the opposite sex.

Lawrence, Lorenzo "spell" religion.

Very rainy days at one time were felt to be the heavens weeping in remorse for their cruelties, though necessary.

Trouble with the metatarsal arch of the foot recalls Saul of Tarsus, and a legendary charade by medical great-grandfather. He and another man walked on stage from opposite sides, shook hands and walked off, twice. Words: met-a-physician, metaphor. Bishop's mitre, something to do with Mithras and his cap.

A car out of the window, MMM. . . . nice? Of course one can have fun with car registration letters, but it becomes too much of a habit. How often one has vowed unsuccessfully not to read every advertisement as one walks down the street?

Nuts is generally recognised as a word for the mad: and how like the human brain is the kernel of a walnut with its two halves and its convolutions.

Chin, and china in the kitchen – China. One supposes Gurdjieff's great Chinese twin brothers (*A&E* p 841) must be Confucius and Lao-Tse, though interest is aroused for other famous brothers such as William and Henry James or the brothers Grimm, collectors of that treasure, the Fairy Tales. Question: How can the Chinese have dictionaries without an alphabetical order in which to arrange them? Answer by Hong Kong friend – the signs are classified under the number of strokes.

Jar can be Jah, iah, short for Jehovah, and as ia,ya can be useful in puns as it is so short, like el, another name for God. O, Os, or(is) mouth can also be played with because they are short, Ophelia.

Orange – angel at the door.

Umbrella stands for sky or heaven; knife for discrimination, like the chopper of Prince Wen Hui's cook which never needed sharpening because he knew so exactly where to cut; (quoted in *Values*). Glue is sex for joining families together, not to be squandered; but these are symbols, not sound-puns. Honey is also for sex, sweetness, easily deceptive.

A dream whose content was "both sexes have beards under the table" opened one's eyes to sexual symbolism: bushes, forests, thickets, narrow valleys. For the male organs: carrot, stick, banana, pencil, cigarette, tower, pillar, bread, other parts of the body, as tongue, nose, toe, finger, thumb (Tom Thumb), hand, horn, fish, serpent or snake; cushion, bag, apple, pestle and mortar. For the female orifice and womb: cave, door, hole, bottle, mouth, round O, os, magic cauldron or cooking pot, tent, curtains, rose. Does boot belong here? Sex symbolism seemed to be everywhere. It was a comfort to know that Freud had written about it, and mercifully the obsession faded after a time or sex itself became a symbol, for creation or for affection. The door for birth can also stand for the door of death, the passage into another world.

Three is a number for sex, father, mother, child, or three private parts in humans, the female quadruped having only two openings and birds one. This was supposed to be why G insisted birds were one-brained beings.

Symbol has been an overworked word for the "unconscious" loves them. A number symbolism was worked on and of course was believed to be the real secret one behind all other number symbolisms. It was mostly connected with the body – five for the male with the fifth limb in the centre as on the dice; six for sexual union of two threes; seven had somehow to be female. Nine for the nine apertures of the male body; this is mentioned in Indian scriptures; it depends a bit on how you count them. Twenty is "a man counted to the end" – all the fingers and toes, a number for completeness. Since then one has read accounts of the Pythagorean number symbolism, without mastering it; it is not the same.

The seven day week, that most useful invention for domestic routine and keeping track of the female cycle, is presumably the nearest approximation to the quarters of the moon month. The names comes from the seven moving visible heavenly bodies, Sun, Moon, Mars, Mercury, Jupiter, Venus, Saturn, translated into appropriate local deities. Precise information as to where and when the week arose is hard to come by as it treads on delicate ground, the difficult question of the age of the ten commandments and the origin of the Sabbath. Under Calendar, Greek, is found: "The planetary week is astrological ..... it is not much older than the Christian era, and was never offi classical times (see F.H. Colson, *The Week*, 1926)''. Anyt with a date around 1926 comes under review as a possible s for ideas used by G in his writing, so it could be that if this made a stir, it suggested the structure of his chapter on Art.

This interminable chapter about lawful inexactitudes in Art, which at first seemed such an absurd idea, became increasingly important as one began to find possible examples. ''Legominisms containing information about all kinds of real events which have taken place in the past are transmitted to the conscious beings of succeeding generations through initiates''. (*A&E* p 458) At the Club-of-Adherents-of-Legominism in Babylon it was proposed that Legominisms should be also handed on by inexactitudes of the Law of Sevenfoldness in various arts, to each of which one day of the week was devoted. Saturday was the day-of-mysteries or day-of-the-theatre, with impromptu role-playing, now popular in psychology. Could Punch and Judy be meant for Pontius Pilate and Judas?

An ancient inexactitude is that Pharaoh can be shown with two left hands to suggest that even he was under a higher Authority. This seems to be done in the lovely design on the back of Tutankhamun's throne. The queen approaches the seated king with a gesture of tenderness and respect. Above is the Sun's disk with a tiny hand at the end of each ray, as if there was a special ray for each of us. It was comical to see that in a modern ceramic reproduction the king's bare tummy had been covered by a flowered cloth. It seems possible the idea of male pregnancy is present in this Akhenaton school of art. Akhenaton (Tutankhamun's father-in-law) is a fascinating figure; Thomas Mann makes him Joseph's Pharaoh; one has romantic fancies about his being the world's first monotheist and that after the fall of his religion in Egypt, its priests may have carried it abroad.

Some other numbers: 7 neck vertebrae, 12 ribs, 32 teeth. 29 and 30 are moon numbers, the month, the age of Jesus. What is 40? Half of life, the 40 days of the temptation, the 40 years of the Israelites in the wilderness, Ali Baba and the 40 thieves?

23 was a favourite number standing for "when two or three are gathered together" with sexual echoes. The "law of typicality", 27 different types (*A & E* p 486): could 3 x 9, the triple crucifixion, be relevant? (see below, the ninth hour).

Four is stability, 4 legs, 4 walls, four quarters of the compass. In ***"Gods, Graves & Scholars"***, 1949, C.W. Ceram says that in 1845 Layard found a human-headed winged lion at Nimrud at the palace of Assurnasirpal II, 885 – 859 B.C. "Today we know the figure represents one of the four cardinal points of the compass. According to the Assyrian tradition, Marduk was shown as a winged bull, Nebo as a human being, Nergal as a winged lion, and Ninib as an eagle". One wonders if this was the origin of the symbols used for the four gospel makers, Mathew – man, Mark – lion, Luke – bull, John – eagle.

Eight was taken as a number for death, the meeting point of two worlds, from its shape of two circles touching or because being twice four it could stand for higher dimensions. Since then one has heard that it is used as a symbol for resurrection and this is why fonts are made octagonal. Gurdjieff's Law of Octaves might suggest Octavian, (the emperor Augustus), but his Enneagram pointed to the death of Jesus at the ninth hour and so to understanding of the crucifixion.

Mr. G's remarks about aniline dyes (*A & E* p 429) made one notice a Yugoslav cushion cover in which the yellow stripes wore out first; more recently in some printed cotton it is the yellow that has gone into holes; and it was always the green crayon that broke in sharpening. So one was led to feeling that colours also had their charge of meaning. Red and white was slightly sinister, the blood stained bandage, the hospital Red Cross, red and blue "couleurs de la Vierge". Black and yellow, wasp. Purple stood perhaps for people, and for Porphyry for his striking hiography of Plotinus. Why have purple and mauve become so fashionable?

Grey went by sound, ger (hard g) – "thy stranger that is within thy gates" (Exodus Ch. 20, the commandment on Sabbath observance). Ger is a Semitic word for guest or client, according to the article on Phoenicia. Grey (or gray) also suggests the sound cr in create, bureaucrat; and the portrait of his mother by James McNeill Whistler (1834–1903), all in tones of the colour grey, which might be what G was referring to on *A & E* p 472.

Yellow is a favourite, standing for daffodils, sunshine, hope; alas also for yellow leaves of autumn, yellow skin of old age, but is not that when you need hope most?

Green, often unlucky, was for God's jealousy, green-eyed jealousy. Why should God be jealous? Green is for Nature, Nature is God's wife and he will punish offences against her! Clearly this is not what the commandment means, but still we are punishing ourselves for pollution.

In his chapter on France, Gurdjieff has an original version of "visiting the iniquity of the fathers upon the children" – "if a father likes to ride, though it be but a child's sled, his son must obligatorily be prepared to drag the great village sleigh up the mountain side" (*A & E* p 671). He uses it about the former ruling class of Russia. Visiting the sins of the fathers upon the children unto the third and fourth generation seems also to be a theme of the Greek plays.

A symbol or series of associations started from an early dream about climbing onto the roof of a rattling shaking mill; mill, millstone about his neck, miller's daughter of fairy stories, mill wheel, Catherine wheel, the nightly turning wheel of the stars, the turning zodiac, the wheel of fortune, the mill of God, the grinding of fate.

4. Brain Research

The cave, prehistoric dwelling and womb of Mother Earth for magic paintings and ceremonies, can in addition to sex symbolism also suggest the rib cage with the lungs and heart, traditional seat of feeling, and still more the skull or brain cave, another magic cauldron or mixing bowl. It is said primitive sculptors give their figures enlarged heads because the head is the most important part of a man, and to us it does seem to be from the head that we look out at the world.

Popularisers of modern brain research (Nigel Calder; ***The Mind of Man,*** Robert E. Ornstein; ***The Psychology of Consciousness***) have put out the stimulating idea that the two halves of the brain contain two more or less separable groups of our sometimes conscious functions. At least it appears that in right-handed people the main ***speech*** centres are in the left hemisphere. (The right side of the body is controlled by the left side of the brain, the nerves crossing over as the rays of light do in the lens of the eye.) Reading and writing are presumably subsidiary to speech, using eye and hand in addition. Often in wasteful inner conversation one is even aware of the incipient movement in throat and tongue, a tired feeling which, arousing some guilt, might make one let go and quieten, if the machine were not so set on continuing.

With this left hemisphere verbal function go calculation and logical thinking if and when we are capable of it. To this side at its best would seem to belong the magnificent but unreal glass palaces erected by medieval scholastics and other philosophers and system builders (Marx) on slender foundations of a few abstract key-words.

The right hemisphere of the cortex is concerned more with orientation in space, co-ordinating movements into a pattern of action, handling things (although the right hand is on the left motor strip), the final stages of seeing, and the recognising of objects and people, which does not always bring their name. The cat can find her way about and recognise the people who feed her and provide a fire; it would be interesting to know how she does it without words and names. In some of us there is recognition but not recall; we cannot voluntarily picture the face of an absent person or recall an object accurately. But an image may arise of its own accord, the head may obstinately start "visualising" the doing of some job, perhaps by a method not thought of before; then it seems one had better do the job now; it seems to be as much a sensing of the movements as a picture by the eyes.

Music and drawing are said to be on the right. One may think the laws of correct perspective need some help from the calculating side; one wonders if it could be a virtue of geometry that it needs both sides. Dancers and musicians report the need for daily practice to keep at the peak of skill. There is no "resting on your laurels''. It must be this right half practical side which often has to say to itself ''You can't count'', and had such difficulty calculating whether lunch at 11 a.m. on the Sunday the clocks were changed for summer time would be 10 a.m. or 12 noon by yesterday's time. The ''right brain'' learns the ''hard way'', by making mistakes and getting ''punished'' – then it remembers; and by imitation, picking up gestures. If you want to remember to do something you ''impress'' a picture of the place where you will be at that time.

One is all too often talking to oneself internally but it is curious that on the rarer occasions when speech is heard in the head it can carry a feeling of coming from another person, an imaginary companion, presumably through a different part of the brain – like Alice, that curious child who was fond of pretending to be two people. What is heard tends to be brief and sterotyped but practical. ''A good place to stop'', ''Heed warnings'', ''leave that'', ''You can't have it both ways'', ''Reculer pour mieux sauter'', ''Does it matter?'' – or ''Don't you dare!'' – but that is said to it, not by it, ''Staring you in the face and you do not see it''. ''Come off it, Bryn.''

The ''idea'' seems to arrive in some unidentifiable form a moment before the actual words: you see you have started making mistakes, the words emphasise it and generally prove to be good advice, it was time to interrupt the mechanical process and give the computer a chance to switch paths. Sometimes it may be just habit. ''May as well be hung for a sheep as a lamb'' is not so sensible. ''Too late now'', ''Do the next thing'', ''Judge not, that ye be not judged''.

This stereotyped practical right brain character may connect with G's advocacy of popular wisdom and proverbs, and with the efficacy and danger of advertising and political slogans. A favourite proverb, because of a tendency to meanness, is ''Waste not, want not'', which is almost a recipe for ''magic'': if you manage with the minimum, Providence will have to see that what is really essential is always available somehow: the ''last straw'' will save. Discovering new economies or better methods is a kind of sport, enlivening routine: but other jobs seem to be done in the most laborious way possible!

Favourite sayings from seaside schooldays: "You're not the only pebble on the beach", "Paddle your own canoe", "A bad workman blames his tools", "Curiosity killed the cat, Information brought it back". Malicious curiosity for gossip was rightly condemned; only later did one realise that curiosity as the desire to understand things is an essential human characteristic. "What's worth doing is worth doing well" – perfectionism – but now the choice is often between doing it badly or not at all.

Imperfection is indeed almost a trade-mark of "their" activity. They use spoiled lives, new things mostly have to get themselves "christened" by a tear (rent, hole) or a stain, the visitors' mugs are all chipped or glued but usable, and jumble and rubbish are most useful. When something is really worn to rags, it finds an immediate new use, padding for a chair-seat perhaps. Very little reaches the compost heap. Old paintings often show the Holy Family in a ruined building; it must be a legominism. Gurdjieff makes the ending of animal sacrifice the theme of Beelzebub's second descent to planet Earth; at first one thought it irrelevant to modern problems but then began to see that sacrifice is still demanded from us. If we can find and offer truly acceptable sacrifices will we be spared so much involuntary suffering? The longing for more "bon-ton" style in this scrappy writing produces a new association, to the Bön, the pre-Buddhist Tibetan religion.

A newspaper definition formerly quoted with approval by stepmother was: "A gentleman is someone who uses the butterknife when alone". The sentiment is arguable (though it is a pity gentleness is no longer held up as admirable), but it illustrates the way concrete images stick in the head. This one often emerges as a crumby knife cuts into the half-pound packet at breakfast.

A more important test of a gentleman is Bernard Shaw's, quoted by Dean Inge: "Try to put into the common stock as much as you take out". G's fourth striving (*A & E* p 386) says "the striving from the beginning of their existence to pay for their arising and their individuality as quickly as possible, in order afterwards to be free to lighten as much as possible the Sorrow of our COMMON FATHER." Repaying the debt of one's arising was a startling idea at first, but one came to see its justice. The right to vote could be made something to be ***earned*** by national service!

The cult of relics was abused in the Middle Ages but we do put relics of famous men in museums. The Russian cult of Lenin's tomb is striking in a materialist ideology. Old or hand-made possessions evoke the people who gave them or from whom they were inherited, and, like old buildings, have more "being", or food for associations, than most new machine-made purchases. The elegant emptiness of modern interior decoration is pleasing in the magazines, but a clutter of books and things-to-do is more homely.

Thinking by symbols and analogies may be good for the education of this "right half" – as also the learning of handicrafts and the care of "things", so that one can come to a richer kind of thinking than just with logical verbal abstractions. Presumably the best mental functioning involves the use of more of the mechanisms together, or with more "light" or more "fuel". But mistakes and inefficiencies are instructive: the thread of connection breaks, you find yourself wondering what you came to this corner to do and have to retrace your steps mentally or physically to find the thread again. Some of the new knowledge about the brain comes from the misfortunes of people with head injuries.

Descartes' "I think, therefore I am" does not seem so self-evident. Thinking is a slippery thing and needs to come back to solid facts, like related dates in history, our need for food and shelter and to rear (and civilise) a new generation, neither too few nor too many; and the inevitability of death. Sometimes one feels God had to create the world to see how his thoughts worked out in practice; and we are just the actors in his theatre. One thinks he plays chess with himself, his right hand not knowing what the left is doing; but perhaps he does want the right hand or "good" forces to win in the end, when they have developed and become conscious through the battle.

Though the locating of functions on the cortex (rind or bark:

the surface) may be new, the division into two is not; in the *Arousing of Thought* (*A & E* p 15) Mr. G says "man has in general two kinds of mentation; one kind, mentation by thought, in which words, always possessing a relative sense, are employed; and the other kind, which is proper to all animals as well as to man, which I would call 'mentation by form'". (image).

So is the right half the Unconscious? It seems not, though perhaps more open to it; dreams are in scenes and movements rather than words. Nor is it necessarily the same as Gurdjieff's so useful concept of the "moving centre" and bodily knowledge. The cerebellum, the little brain at the back of the head, corresponds well with his "mechanical part of the moving centre"; it looks after acquired movements that become automatic, all the things that a baby learns and an adult takes for granted until they go wrong: grasping, using eye and hand together, balance, walking, pronouncing sounds; and parts of later acquired skills like swimming, cycling, typing.

For the "instinctive centre" one reads of deeper, earliest-evolved parts of the brain regulating breathing, heart, temperature, thirst, digestion, excretion, pleasure, sex, laughter .... which are mostly outside our conscious control though the yogi may be different. Here too are the mechanisms for generating emotion, when something from outside closely concerns the body's needs or security, via the sympathetic (? unsympathetic since it is used for fighting) nervous system and the chemical hormones secreted by glands. However parts of the cortex are also involved in emotion. In the brain stem there is a centre controlling waking and attention, another for drowsiness and sleep, and a special switch for dreams; if the movements mechanism were not disconnected we should all be sleep-walkers.

It is interesting that inhibition (stopping) is much favoured in the operation of brain cells, "otherwise we should have an epileptic fit every time we opened our eyes". Sometimes there is too much light, too much stimulus, one wants to do too many things at once as in dishing up lunch, and it is necessary to say "one thing at a time". One hears of a new American diagnosis for children's problems – "hyperkinetic", restless, unable to concentrate, from too much stimulation by television and food additives. However "love getting too excited" said young Tessa; and the teenagers "high" must be rather similar. And the children like playing ghosts or visiting the dark cellar and pretending to be frightened; and frightening films and stories are exciting; it must be a question of degree, not like a paralysing fear. One kind of happiness is the release of a flow of energy, but you cannot have that all the time.

An educational precept: "Hear and forget; see and remember, do and understand", gives a feeling of the different functionings.

The study of centres is recommended as the beginning of self-observation; the idea of the two halves stimulated a fresh start. "I never seem to be able to get a good repeatable observation", cried Madge at a group meeting. But perhaps that is the point, our self-observation is not static and repeatable like a physical experiment: perhaps it never will fit completely into any theoretical scheme. This may be because we are such complex machines or it may be because our experience is flowing and is already partly in eternity. A sharp clear observation is a gift, if not from a "guardian angel" at least from a better state of consciousness; you have learned that, it is printed in experience and available for future self-management. Next time you must go further.

June 1974. A vain hunt for the Anthroposophical Stern-kalender on "The Week" had produced instead some colour reproductions. Looking at Botticelli's "Spring" over early tea, the drinker thought the composition rather naïve, just a row of figures. But who is this Madonna-like central figure, with hand raised against a background of bushes, red and white drapery and Cupid flying overhead? The drinker had long had difficulty joining heads and necks in drawing and had begun to notice real artists didn't always do so well either. This Venus of Botticelli's also has her head on one side at an uncomfortable angle. Suppose the convention is at least sometimes an intentional inexactitude? What could it mean? Perhaps she is "listening to the other side". In Luke's Good Samaritan parable the priest and the Levite passing by on the other side may just be the other side of the road, but not for nothing is "the other side" a favourite expression for the invisible kingdom, or the other side of the curtain, or of the river of death.

But does it go with a section on brain research? Maybe it can. Our heads are receiving sets, they are able to learn to listen consciously. This is where the experience of observing mental processes helps. What arises from inside is fainter and drowned by too much "noise" from outside; and you have to wait for when it wants to come. On the other hand it looks as though the invisible can use us unconsciously any time it wants but that may be in ways we shall regret later. It may be that the "radio sets" also sometimes transmit without knowing it.

* * * * * * *

In view of exercises to divide attention it is odd that in tracking back to see why a breakage happened, a split in attention is often found. Hesitation foxes the moving centre. "Don't talk to the man at the wheel".

18th January 1975: After writing diary, climb out of bed, the poncho sweeps empty mug and saucer off the desk. The all-purpose saucer, used seven times every day, is split in half. That was a lapse of attention. There was one more of these saucers. In the confusion of removal eight years ago, when there was nowhere to put anything down, it was stood for making tea on the new self-igniting gas cooker. The wrong tap was turned and lit the gas under it; it got a ring crack and was put aside.

19th January. Have to use the cracked one for now. At bedtime, reaching down the milk saucepan from the cooker hood, think "ought to be more careful about the poncho/does that cat really need feeding again" and watch helplessly as the other pan is dislodged and smashes the second saucer. "Now what you going to do?" says head. Upsetting but also comical. Too neatly done to be "just accident". Both saucers, two days running; each time the mug escaped..

George's Christmas present Napoleon-ivy tea-cup (design used on St. Helena) has survived two years, touch wood; perhaps it would be safe to take some nicer china. Over the next days several hunts in the drawers of inherited china to replace that saucer with two others and a plate; work out a new routine and parking place.

The survival of George's cup is felt as possibly "paid for" by an accident when he was a boy in which the handle of a valuable looking blue and white antique coffee pot was broken. He was scolded: "Maybe you feel you couldn't help it, but you could be sorry it happened". But to the coffee pot has also been attributed the safety so far of a small size, also blue and white, Victorian wash stand ewer, used for watering the geraniums in the window.

5. *Youth and Age.*

John Ruskin (1819 – 1900), a person much loved in his old age, wrote in the preface to "Sesame and Lilies": "Work while you have light, especially while you have the light of morning, There are few things more wonderful to me than that old people never tell young ones how precious their youth is." William James in "Talks to Teachers" said: "Could the young but realize how soon they will become mere walking bundles of habits, they would give more heed to their conduct while in the plastic state ....Every smallest stroke of virtue and vice leaves its never-so-little scar ....(If a youth) keep faithfully busy ....he can count on waking up some fine morning to find himself one of the competent ones of his generation."

Dean Inge in "More Lay Thoughts of a Dean" says a valuable self-mastery "is the power of switching off thoughts at will. I have always found this extremely difficult, especially thoughts of anger. It is supremely important, because our thoughts almost literally ***cut grooves for themselves*** in the mind. The grooves get deeper and deeper, and our thoughts flow in them more and more irresistibly, till our judgement is quite warped. Nursing a grudge in this way is most pernicious, especially when we rehearse to ourselves the scathing rejoinder which we could make if we liked. Sooner or later out come these crushing retorts and we have made an enemy for life."

Often repeated opinions and conversations must also cut grooves. Talkativeness is called a fault of the old (and of the female!) perhaps it is a need. It must be admitted that although some tiredness is blank, another sort of tiredness leads to verbal tapes running automatically and too fast, in speech or internally, without one having the kind of energy which could check them even when one does for a moment notice what is happening.

One the other hand it seems good sometimes to revive and refresh old memories, recall the people and places we have known, not to lose the past; but these are more complete images, not just verbal grooves. During or just after the war Mr. Bennett gave us a task to take each day one calendar year of our lives and remember all we could. It was hard to recall much by years, but the idea of cultivating memories took root. The brain researchers distinguish short and long term memory and find a special centre whose damage prevents long term imprinting. Factors for imprinting should be emotion, or novelty arousing interest, also repetition and long familiarity, but excessive painfulness (shell-shock) causes loss of memory, and too much novelty at once cannot be absorbed.

William James quotes Galton finding from members of the Royal Society that as men get older they use visual images less and words more; and Darwin writing that love of poetry, music and pictures seemed to have atrophied from disuse and his mind (seemed to have) become a kind of machine for grinding general laws out of large collections of facts, (but notice he was aware of it).

One recalls that day-dreams in youth were about emotionally satisfying situations; day-dreaming does apparently belong to early life and, though censured, can show something about what one wants from the future. One dream, caught in the canteen, is recallable; it made the boss's wife die of measles, so one could be stepmother to her children – she, who managed to become a genuine friend to her husband's former employee.

Poets who die young are naturally mourned, yet it is the energy of youth which produces the lyrical outpouring, and scientists and philosophers may do their most original work in their twenties.

What *is* the difference between an old person and a young one? What gain can one show from the passage of the years to set against the loss of youth? One had sneaking thoughts that old people were fossils, cardboard, only young people were really alive; partly perhaps it was a defence against admitting that oneself must eventually die (still can't) so one did not want to identify with people who were nearing it.

Now one sees the other side of the coin and feels a bit jealous of the young: and clutches at a saying like "young people not have very much inside, so not much to observe yet" (Fritz Peters, *"Gurdjieff Remembered"* p 27). "I tell many times that if wish to observe self must start from outside, by observing movements of body", "all work must start with body", and a warning, "Europeans have already formed inner self that makes them rotten inside because formed with unconsciousness", (ibid.)

Jung studied the different stages of life, the child discovering and defending his ego, the young adult having to find a place in the world, earn a living, marriage; Jung's view was that for psychological health in the second half of life religion and a belief in immortality were necessary.

There is a story from the Eddas of Thor's visit to Giantland shere the Giant King played magic tricks, of which one was to taunt Thor into wrestling with the old nurse, who defeated him; afterwards the king confessed to the humiliated Thor that the old woman was Old Age, of whom no one ever got the better. Carlos Castaneda's Indian sorcerer Don Juan said there were four enemies for the man seeking to be a man of knowledge: fear, clarity, power and old age.

The beer slogan "Get Younger every day" is peculiarly cheering, and an old person can be spoken of as "young in mind". Uncle at 80 got out the atlas to look up places in the news. One may fight against old age, try to keep flexible; the brain responds to exercise, mental and also physical which improves the circulation. A picture comes back of the colonel's aged widow, still upright and handsome in rustling black silks and silver chains: there is courage in it. One does discover a wish to leave something behind, a sense of urgency in case there are not many more years.

Some apparently unremarkable people manage to return to

memory quite often. One comes by her way of sweeping up crumbs with a pan and hand broom, another by her name – little old Miss Webb – by association with spiders and weaving. She cleaned our flat in war-time, sister-in-law of George the Express Dairy Stable man. The sisters belonged to some sect of Brethren and Miss Webb's way of stopping her employer doing laundry on Sunday, the only free day, was to take it home and do it herself, a form of preaching that was appreciated. Old George liked his beer and perhaps found the preaching more trying, but their tiny rooms over the stables and the air raid shelter were kept gleaming.

At the time of looking for a first job it was maddening to be told "You need experience". How were you to get experience unless someone gave you a job? Obviously the older person should have acquired some wisdom from experience, from living through a chunk of history, from seeing how lives turn out over the years. "Integration," like "subjective and objective," is a word that took a long time to acquire meaning, but a useful one for describing maturity. Experience, ideas about life and the world, and all the many I's, should be properly connected up into a whole.

At any age one can only "use the NOW." When one is not able to work because the energy is not there, one can only wait, knowing that in the past it has always returned. Sufferings and frustrations have proved to have a purpose. So one may hope that when "the lawful infirmities of old age" (*A & E* p 364) finally get the upper hand, the light burns dim, and one becomes "hopeless idiot" in this life, the same process of Good Friday and Easter Sunday will operate into eternity. With us in the North the Christ child is born in ***winter.***

In the New Model, Ouspensky writes under Experimental Mysticism, p 340, about the "long body" of man from birth to death, called Linga Sharira in Indian philosophy. The real self is not just at this point in time, either young or old; the child or young person we were is still part of us and it is this whole life long body we should find waiting for us in eternity.

Complete editions of Grimm's Fairy Tales include a bitter but hard-to-forget fable, the Duration of Life. When God created the world, the ass, the dog and the monkey complained their life was hard, to live thirty years was too long, so the Lord had pity and took some away. But man, joyous, healthy and vigorous, said that at thirty he had built his house and planted fruit trees and was just intending to enjoy himself. So man's first thirty years are his human years; he is merry, works with pleasure and is glad of his life. Then he is given eighteen years of the donkey's burden-bearing, carrying the corn which feeds others, with blows and kicks for reward; then come twelve years of the dog lying in the corner and growling, having no longer any teeth to bite with; last are the monkey's ten years when man does silly things and becomes the butt of children.

For a more cheerful view, set against this story Gurdjieff's injunction to prepare for yourself a happy old age (*R.M.* p 39) – for which good personal relationships are obviously one ingredient.

6. Mind and Brain

Back to that tiresome inner talkativeness: a Reader's Digest article of August 1971 on Relaxation and the work of Dr. Edmund Jacobson, says "If you relax your tongue, lips and throat it is impossible to think in words". It seems to be true, but how long can you keep it up, just when you need it most? "You must have gold to make gold", Work while you are able, for "the night cometh when no man may work". (John 9.4 & 12.35).

The article says "You can't sleep because something is on your mind and you can't turn your brain off. But your brain is *not* your mind". That is just the point one beats against in brain research. Is the mind something more than the brain? It does feel as if it was So much of the brain is allocated to specific functions controlling the body that there does not seem much room in it for mind. Sometimes one has mind, it is alive, kindled, an energy is flowing. But all too often the mind or brain is heavy. It reads without comprehension and blames the author, it can't stop repetitive talking to itself, it can't tackle its task, the energy is not there to use.

21st June 1974. Cloudless sky on midsummer day, a green garden to spend it in, syringa blossom at its brief peak of perfection; the beautiful moment has to be used for this writing. The relation between brain and mind, between physical body and a higher counterpart? Is it that when energy in the cells rises above a certain level it can flow together as a whole; or bridge the gap between the material brain and the structure that is there in the invisible dimension but only sometimes consciously contactable?

When people said at meetings that they wanted more energy they were answered: "What would you do with it? Waste it or even use it harmfully?" One can recognise some of the conditions which have released a flow of energy, one knows it cannot last very long so it is precious. Does the energy have to be held a little still, not used for immediate enjoyment, so that it can go over into eternity, feed the invisible structure or prepare another step? . . .

Rude awakening. All that hot afternoon the milk was sitting in the sun by the front door. Does mind forget the housekeeping for the bit of poetry? Later as one walked up the two stone steps, reading the paper and "asleep", feeling some laziness had been earned, the new Oxfam sandals caught . . . headlong crash . . . flat on the ground. Rueful inspection of damage, only grazes. Punishment for pride, payment, a joke? The stupidity about the milk has been confessed, there's no need to put in the fall.

But perhaps there is. At the peak of seeming consciousness, though vividly aware of the sunlit scene, there was certainly no sense of other worlds or other dimensions. And yet there had been something, a fleeting idea, almost a whispering in the air, that Bruin might be responsible for today's piece. His name was noted in the margin as a reminder.

R. L. Brown, mathematician and long-time friend, died two summers ago of a tumour of the pituitary, so naturally he was in one's mind in these days of trying to write about brain anatomy, so presumptious for an amateur. At around age 30 he and M. W. Thring worked with J. G. Bennett on "the physics", a paper for the Royal Society about eternity . . . gosh, the reprint is still actually in the souvenir drawer – volume 198, 1948 . . . about a *five*-dimensional manifold and freely falling observers. Bruin had said it would be worth going on with that work.

The paper "Unified field theory in a curvature-free five-dimensional manifold" starts with the imperceptibility of the fifth dimension – eternity or "anti-time". Imperceptible, invisible, intangible, and yet it seems to be there. In *The Dramatic Universe* Mr. Bennett adds a sixth dimension "Hyparxis", but one has never attempted to understand it and skips all equations, not even knowing the mathematical symbols. Presumably others do the some. Has one really to try to examine all that? Mind, where are you? In the fable one was delighted at finding how to evade the question by reference to the best physicists. Koestler has written about them.

Waking at five, the morning after recopying this piece on Friday 13th September, head is trying to formulate that memory, reviving the image of that midsummer afternoon, is a further element to be brought into the mind-brain question. So is the framework of will, wanting to complete this writing, which has grown from a short piece suggested nearly a year ago by a visitor's account of watching for flying saucers at Warminster. She has Mother's maiden initials D.W. This started a pondering because of family connections with Warminster. "If people are so keen on flying saucers, why not give them one?" Only much later was it seen as a repeat of Gurdjieff's Space-ship Karnak theme for *All and Everything*.

7. *Higher Bodies and the Face on the Moon*

At a group meeting in Petersburg in 1916 someone asked Gurdjieff about reincarnation and whether it was possible to believe in cases of communication with the dead. "Many things are possible", said G. "But it is necessary to understand that man's being, both in life and after death, if it does exist after death, may be very different in quality". (In Ouspensky's *In Search of the Miraculous, Fragments of an Unknown Teaching*, p. 31)

Quality of being needs fusion, inner unity or "crystallisation", which is only obtained by friction, by the struggle of yes and no; and the crystallisation can be on a wrong foundation. "Remember you come here having already understood the necessity of struggling with yourself – only with yourself. Therefore thank everyone who gives you an opportunity''. This hard saying was one of the aphorisms painted up in the Study House at Gurdjieff's Institute for the Harmonious Development of Man, near Fontainebleau. They are translated in ''Views from the Real World – Early Talks of Gurdjieff'', Routledge and Kegan Paul, printed in the USA.

At a later meeting in Petersburg, G said that, according to an ancient teaching, a fully developed man consists of four bodies, each controlling the lower one, but he is *not* born with the finer bodies (Fragments p 40). On the other hand, turning to that old favourite the Food Diagram, or man as a chemical factory, with the possibility of two conscious shocks to increase the production of finer matters, one reads on page 194 that our two higher centres are fully developed and properly functioning; it is the lower centres that are undeveloped and so cannot connect with them.

Which ancient teachings give man four bodies or divide him into four parts, cart, horse, driver, master? It is not very clear that the chariot metaphor in the Katha Upanishad is a fourfold division. In the Hermetic ''The Key'' man is given five parts, mind, reason, soul, spirit and body, and Mead in ''Thrice Greatest Hermes'' compares it specifically with the Katha Upanishad. Plato's chariot metaphor in the Phaedrus stresses that man's horses are unequal, one noble, one ignoble. There is a chariot in the ''Definitions of Asklepios'' but here the sun is the charioteer. The King in his chariot makes a beautiful subject for ancient art, as on Tutankhamun's casket.

Jung likes to divide us into four parts, and speaks of the quaternion (cross?). From sensation, feeling and thought he separates intuition as the fourth. (Glossary, ''***Memories, Dreams Reflections***'').

In the final chapter of ***All and Everything, "From the Author"***, G compares man to a hackney carriage, broken-down horse and cabby. The fourth part ''I'', who should be the owner, is in us any temporary passenger. The connections – shafts and reins – add complexity. Carriage, horse and coachman here are body, feelings, thoughts, three parts present in every man rather than higher bodies. To reconcile these ideas theoretically one may perhaps say that when these functions are fully organised they become higher bodies. One has heard the second body called the body of feeling.

* * * * * * *

Dion Fortune (where did she get that striking pseudonym?) said emotion is a force of an electrical nature. This seems to "explain" many miracles. Questions of energies are subtle.One would dearly like to be able to correlate self-observations with physiology, but they keep escaping. Even the use of the words thought, feeling and sensation as authenticating a three-fold division is accepted with insufficient question. They are in a way all body; thought is sensed as in the head or sometimes in the tongue; emotions are recognised by their effects on the body, as particular kinds of sensation. That "feel" can be loosely used for both emotion and sensation may be an advantage.

G wrote in 1927 that he could concentrate life-forces of such compactness as to put to sleep an elephant or kill a yak a mile away, but he still could not remember himself with people once the prepared energy was used up, so he resolved to forgo the use of his powers of telepathy and hypnotism save in defined circumstances.

The Tibetan yak in this pasage sticks in memory, though one does not see the use of the accomplishment. Madame Alexandra David-Neel, extraordinary Frenchwoman who died in 1969 aged 101, wrote in ***Magic and Mystery in Tibet*** (Corgi) about Tibetan "psychic sports"; these are long distance trance-walking, which reminds one of seven-league boots, generating internal heat in the snow, and telepathy or sending messages "on the wind", all of use in Tibetan conditions.

In 1911 she saw a blessing ceremony by the Dalai Lama, who had taken refuge at Kalimpong; she was interested in a Naljorpa, a tramp or travelling ascetic with magic powers, who seemed to be mocking the ceremony. In the afternoon she visited "this Himalayan Diogenes" at the monastery where he was staying. "What is this idiot here for?" asked the vagabond. The interpreter was embarrassed, but Mme David-Neel knew that in India also certain yogins insult anyone who approaches. "For a blessing to be efficacious, he who gives it must possess the power that he professes to communicate", and "to fashion stars out of dog-dung, that is the Great Work", the Naljorpa said in answer to her questions.

* * * * * * *

"Thou shalt love the Lord thy God with all thy heart, and with all thy soul, and with all thy mind, and with all thy strength" (Mark ch. 12) is a four-fold division and could be the outline of a psychology, taking strength as the body or possibly the will, but subject to another question one always needs to ask, what is meant by soul in this particular context?

In ***The Law of Psychic Phenomena,*** Chicago 1893, Thomas Jay Hudson wrote: "The objective mind is the physical brain and dies with it", but "The perfect memory of the subjective mind – or soul – argues for the retaining of identity after death". He equates the subjective mind (or in later terminology, the unconscious) with the soul, which is interesting. However it may be added one has read that where "the perfect recall" of hypnosis can be checked, it is found to include a good deal that is invented.

An alternative for "the Lord thy God" is "your ideal, what you care about most". Too often it is mammon.

Verifying the quotation produced something interesting. The original version in Deuteronomy 6.5 has only three: "Thou shalt love the Lord thy God with all thine heart, and with all thy soul, and with all thy might." Mind has been added in the New Testament. Luke chapter 10 has the same four as Mark, but Matthew 22 has three, heart, soul and mind.

The Theosophists even give man in all seven parts or bodies, (Claude Falls Wright: ***Modern Theosophy,*** Boston 1894) and Gurdjieff in ***"Fragments"*** did give us seven centres.

* * * * * * *

This person cannot say how many higher bodies or parts man may have, being only concerned with hoping there is or will be *something* which can continue after physical death, and with looking for ideas or observations which could relate to it. Such are integration and control, and a physical body which can be made to do what it does not like, get up in the morning when the alarm goes, a skilled servant, Brother Ass trained, obedient, taken care of and given its due rewards and treats. But physical body itself is also a teacher. A feature of these experiences has been, not the high states or ecstasies promised by the mystics, but that it is *low* states which are productive, or precede or pay for a discovery, though a spell of joy may follow.

There is a certain charge of elitism against G's teaching, particularly in its earlier form. One feels G said immortality was only for the few who could earn it, because he needed pupils who could work exceptionally hard. People who are in a position to do that can open up opportunities for others. One feels also that G had a great compassion for "the ordinary idiot", and that his real hope was to benefit the many through the prepared few, but how?

This person is inclined to the more common view that there is immortality of some sort for all or most people. One answer for the ordinary man may be in the importance of "belonging", in spirit if not outwardly, to a family, a group, a neighbourhood, a country; of loving and serving something bigger than yourself. The "solidarity" of a Trade Union or a religion would be a virtue if it were not directed against the other groups; then it becomes extended selfishness, even self-pity. If Everyman will do his best with the duties and opportunities he does have, he will share in the immortality of larger unities. Loneliness in the next world must be horrible.

Is there not a discipline in a life-time of daily work properly carried out, delivering letters or milk, or collecting rubbish, selling bread or vegetables, looking after water supplies or drains? Such a character was the grandmother laundry-driver, "Ducks", valued by customers for her cheerfulness, who saw one on her knees polishing the floor and joked as she shouldered the heavy basket, "Say one for me while you're down there".

* * * * * * *

In *All and Everything* we get a shock from reading of a first and second death. Death is called the sacred Rascooarno, for which the interpretation Heavenly Body, Heavenly Flesh, given earlier may perhaps be accepted.

Sometimes one meets the idea of a first death during this life, "Die before you die." This dying is conversion, dying to the old man, the start of a new way of looking at life; it may also be a dying which is to be constantly repeated, detachment, a dying daily, letting go an automatic urge, waking up. G uses it in this way at the end of ***"From the Author"*** (p 1232) when he writes of a death spoken of in all religions, which can occur even during life, and is "the first liberation of man".

An early aphorism of Gurdjieff's ran something like this: "It is possible to be born again, but in order to be born again you must first die; and before you can safely die it is advisable to wake up". One has never been quite sure what G meant by waking up apart from a brief increase of consciousness or coming into one's presence. One has heard it connected with "Watch" in the exhortation "Watch and pray". In this aphorism one could say it emphasises the importance of preparation; without that rebirth might be madness . . . Found it, ***Fragments*** p 217 – 219, where the aphorism is not quite in the same form. Waking up is given as seeing one's own nothingness.

"Twice-born" can also be thought to mean the dead. Death is seen by analogy as birth into a new world as much greater than ours, as our daylight world is than the womb.

However throughout the main part of ***All and Everything,*** G makes the first sacred Rascooarno the death of the physical body, with a second death later. When we have passed the fearful obstacle, the exam, of dying, we are still not safely home. If enough work has not been done, there has to be more self-perfecting and a purging away of faults. Purgatory seems such a sensible idea, even if not in Scripture, that the Protestants would have done better to take it over from the Catholics, though hardly in the form that repeating so many prayers can literally buy off so many days in Purgatory.

Through all the chapters in which Beelzebub on the space-ship is educating his favourite grandson, man is represented not as having four bodies or seven centres, but according to a simpler three-fold scheme. Man is a three-brained being in a planetary body which has the possibility of "coating" two further bodies, as if one were placed within the other (p 764), the body Kesdjan and the Higher Being Body or body of the soul.

A similar scheme dividing man into three parts, with successive deaths of the two lower parts, is found in Plutarch (c.A.D. 45 - 120) in his dialogue "On the Face which appears in the Orb of the Moon". (Loeb translation by Harold Cherniss of Princeton, 1957)

The first part of the dialogue is a mixture of science – a rational discussion of eclipses, the laws of reflection and the visual ray which was thought to go out from the eye – with sophistry: Is the moon habitable? If so, why don't we see men falling headlong, tumbling off the moon? Plutarch has some fun with paradoxes of "up" and "down" which ensue if the earth is a sphere. "If a man should so coalesce with the earth that its centre is at his navel" he would have his feet "up" and his head "up" at the same time. Footnote: "The most famous later parallel is the position of Lucifer in Dante's Inferno" – where by a fine insight on reaching the very depths of Hell, Satan himself, in the centre of the earth, a somersault sets the traveller rapidly climbing up the other side.

Then Plutarch gives the myth learned from a stranger who shared the thirty years service by holy men on an island west of Britain, where Kronos, father of Zeus, is confined in a magic sleep and tended by daimones – here translated spirits – who manifest themselves not only by dreams and omens, but openly in visions and voices. Afterwards the stranger visited Carthage and "discovered certain sacred parchments that had been secretly spirited off to safety when the earlier city was being destroyed and had lain unnoticed in the ground for a long time."

The stranger said we should specially honour the moon, sovereign over life and death, and home of Phersephone. It is usually spelt Persephone, could this be anything to do with G's Phu-phu-kle? (A & E p 803). The encyclopaedia says various forms of the name are found.

Man is composed not of two parts but of three, body, psyche translated soul and nous, translated here as mind, but by another writer translated as spirit. However two intermediate parts could make man fivefold, for "the result of soul and body commingled is the irrational (alogon) or affective factor, whereas of mind and soul the conjunction produces reason; and of these the former is the source of pleasure and pain, the latter of virtue and vice."

Earth furnishes man's body, the moon his soul and the sun his mind. In the first death Demeter on earth dissociates the soul from the body swiftly and violently. The souls wander in the region between earth and moon, unjust souls paying penalties while the good souls pass a set time in the gentlest part of the air, called "the meads of Hades", in the earth's shadow, to purge away pollutions contracted from the body. Then like exiles brought home they reach the moon with joy and excitment. They receive crowns (stephanois) of feathers because they have made the irrational or feeling part of the soul orderly and tolerably tractable to reason.

The spirits (daimones) descend to earth to take charge of oracles, attend the highest mystic rituals, ward off or chastise misdeeds, and flash forth as saviours in war or at sea. If they act unjustly they are again confined in human bodies. On the moon the mind is slowly and gently detached from the soul, "separated by love for the image in the sun through which shines forth manifest the desirable and fair and divine and blessed towards which all nature in one way or another yearns", and the sun takes back the mind which he gave. "In fact the self of each of us is not anger or fear or desire just as it is not bits of flesh or fluids either but that with which we reason and understand". "For the inanimate is itself powerless and susceptible to alien agents, and the mind is impassible and sovereign; but the soul is a mixed and intermediate thing, even as the moon has been created by god a compound and blend of the things above and below."

Why should Plutarch's essay be worth so much attention? Is there something hidden which one has missed? There were barbaric sayings in the "system" as taught by Ouspensky: "the dead go to the moon'', ''make moon in yourself''. A minor point: Plutarch twice mentions inflated skins which recall Gurdjieff's bourdiouks in ***Remarkable Men*** (pp 214 and 224), when they killed the goats to make floats and buffers for a raft.

Carthage was a ''New Town'' founded in the 9th century B.C. by those commercially talented Semites and sailors the Phoenicians, who are also called Canaanites. Their language was closely allied to Hebrew. Until the Roman destruction in 146 B.C. Carthage had an important temple of Eshmun, identified with Asklepios, saviour and healer. Under Greek influence Baal-Ammon or Moloch was represented with ram's horns on his forehead or with a scythe.

Association suggests looking up in an illustrated history of France the Gaulish bronze head (Musée de Saint Germain) of Cernunnos, the horned god of night (horns for the moon), of death, evil and underground riches. The head is impressive. Mythology calls up many rich connections, but imprecise.

In the same ''Histoire de France Illustree'' by Albert Malet is a story of the barbaric and bloody feud between two queens, Brunehaud, wife of the Merovingian King Sigebert, and Frédégonde, wife of his brother, King Chilperic. Finally in 613 Frédégonde's son had Brunehaud, then 70, tied to the tail of an unbroken horse. It sounds like a historical original of the Siegfried or Sigurd and Brynhild story, which acquired mythical elements as it travelled north. The frustrated love and the magic sleep in the ring of flames have a more symbolic meaning, and may have suggested the image of Sleeping Beauty in her bramble-surrounded castle.

Perhaps after all Plutarch's formulation, to make one's feelings and impulses ''tolerably tractable to reason'' is a better psychological aim than either blind materialism or the ascetic's total withdrawal and condemnation of life. It is the fourth way, remaining in the world but not of it. Life in the world provides the experiences and duties to be wrestled with. In the dialogue on why the oracles at Delphi were no longer given in verse but in plain prose, the maxims of the wise men inscribed there: ''Know thyself'' and ''Avoid extremes'' are quoted as examples of brevity. They are still valuable. Delphi was near Plutarch's home town of Chaeronea where he set up a school. He spent some years in Rome and did visit Egypt.

The volume with the moon dialogue also contains two short pieces both called "De Esu Carnium" (scholars like quoting the titles in Latin) "Peri Sarkophagias" or "On the Eating of Flesh". Plutarch in his youth, like Seneca, followed the Pythagoreans' advocacy of vegeterianism, which is not a modern invention. Here he writes vividly, it reminds one of "the roast and boiled corpses" of Gurdjieff's priest Abdil (*A & E* p 202). Abdil's planetary body was hacked to pieces.

Plutarch ends the first of these discourses: "The stories told about the sufferings and dismemberment of Dionysus and the outrageous assaults of the Titans upon him, and their punishment... after they had tasted his blood – all this is a myth which in its inner meaning has to do with rebirth. For to that faculty in us which is unreasonable and disordered and violent, and does not come from the gods but from evil spirits, the ancients gave the name Titans, that is to say those that are punished and subject to correction." A footnote describes this as a "Greek equivalent of original sin".

Dionysus – the name may mean son of god – who is the same as Bacchus, can also be represented as a horned god. Michelangelo's tipsy Bacchus has horns broken off short.

In the "Isis and Osiris" Plutarch discusses the myth of the dismemberment of Osiris: "the soul of Osiris is everlasting and imperishable, but his body Typhon oftentimes dismembers and causes to disappear.... Isis wanders hither and yon in her search for it, and fits it together again" – as we have repeatedly to re-collect our being in time.

The conversation on "The Obsolescence of Oracles" is supposed to take place in or shortly before 83–84 A.D., a year of Pythian games. There is mention of the recent death of a prophetic priestess, or as G would say, a pythoness. A traveller returned from Egypt says that at the shrine of Ammon the ever-burning lamp uses less oil every year, which the priests interpret as proof that the years are getting shorter. The company ridicule this as "painting the lion from a single claw". It recalls Gurdjieff's contrary statement in ***"Glimpses of Truth"*** (the earliest account of his teaching, printed in ***"Views from the Real World"***) that with real knowledge of the laws of proportion in the human body a sculptor could build up the whole of Gogol's body from his nose alone.

How is this for more lively writing, "On the Cleverness of Animals"? "Such was the elephant which at Alexandria played the rival to Aristophanes the grammarian. They were, in fact, in love with the same flower girl: nor was the elephant's love the less manifest: as he passed by the market, he always brought her fruit and stood beside her for a long time and would insert his trunk, like a hand, within her garments and gently caress her fair breasts." Those who have read ***"Remarkable Men"*** may see a resemblance to the story of Gurdjieff's dog Philos which brought him Jerusalem artichokes from the market.

G's English story "I not like so much conversation" could recall Plutarch's essay against talkativeness, but the point is put more briefly and powerfully in the little epistle of James Ch. 3: "If any man offend not in word, the same is a perfect man, and able also to bridle the whole body. Behold, we put bits in the horses' mouths, that they may obey us; and we turn about their whole body.... Even so the tongue is a little member, and boasteth great things". What if Plutarch was the author of the epistle? And wrote his own moral essay "Concerning Talkativeness" as a clue or signature?

8. The Holy Planet Purgatory, and more Greek Philosophers

The writing of the previous section, with its too ambitious theme, made itself difficult. Revising it is still giving trouble, it wants to acquire new material. Today, 14th November 1974, a second consecutive rainy day, settle down to work in the morning, must have another try.

Thunder quite near, wind, hail, but bright intervals. Try to look up Food Diagram, again in ***Fragments,*** but don't find it at once from the index. "This is thin, you must read it in Purgatory," Mr. Gurdjieff said once. Purgatory is so difficult, but it seems one must try.

For once there was enough attention available to read the chapter in ***All and Everything*** with some comprehension, to see it as a Creation Epic, with newer astronomy and science and with cosmoses from the Greeks. The ultimate destiny of Tetartocosmoses, who include men, is to be a help to the Creator in the administration of the enlarging world. (p 762)

The first conscious shock, self-remembering and observing impressions as they enter (***Fragments*** p 188 and 193) and the second conscious shock, transformation and transmutation of the emotions (p 192) of the human food factory of G's teaching in 1915 become the conscious labour and intentional suffering of ***All and Everything,*** wider but still two-stage.

The fat and thin monks, at the end of the chapter Purgatory, are the one bit easy to remember. So there really is such a thing as the sublimation or transmutation of the longing of unsatisfied sex, of the sigh; but only on condition of a thirst for self-perfecting, for being, for a higher love. 16th November, a dream, associating to ''A bicycle is what you need.... you can't do it without a loving friend, a friend to love'', so the last six words were added to the preceding sentence; self-perfecting alone is too ego-centred.

At last one seems to catch the meaning of early Christian virginity and celibacy; it was a witness to the possibility of transmutation of sex energy, but the right preliminary conditions are not easily found. As a general rule one would prefer self-restraint and faithfulness in ordinary life, ''waiting for the real thing'' as Mrs. B said once, to life-time vows of abstinence. ''In respect of these being-substances, the beings themselves must always be very, very much on their guard in order to avoid undesirable consequenses for their entire whole'' (***A&E*** p 791).

Higher love is perhaps not so monogamous, so exclusive; not a cupid's arrow but a radiating beacon fed from below. Beware self-deception, we are not yet so sublimated as the angels in heaven!

* * * * * * *

"After you assimilate what I am giving . . . you will take a position of responsibility . . . . For every satisfaction you must accept so much dissatisfaction", Gurdjieff said in a New Year talk recorded by Kathryn Hulme in ***Undiscovered Country,*** p 136. Grown-up, no more receiving without giving! But also, "It is law, for one dissatisfaction, ***always*** there must be one satisfaction" p 103.

"Payment", like the Unconscious, is one of the topics one rubs against again and again, but probably never will be able to "explain" fully. G talked about payment and sheepshearing, and wrote more formally that we have to give off a substance (or vibration) Askokin for the maintenance of the Earth's detached fragments, the moon and Anulios (*A & E* pages 84, 182, 1104-7). What is this "moon"? A "psychic ether", "electricity" for fuelling telepathy and the manifestations of the unconscious? As men have ceased to produce Askokin by conscious labours and intentional suffering, Nature has to extract it by increasing the number of deaths. G gives this as the cause of war.

Is energy drawn off from us, or do we just not produce as much as we would like? Sometimes one would even blame lead in the air, or other poison, for physical discomforts attributed to insufficient energy. In moderation such bodily suffering does serve psychological processes in oneself, preventing overconfidence and dense self-satisfaction, or just giving something to struggle against and separate from, so perhaps generating finer, less tangible energies in due course.

In pages 801 – 2 Gurdjieff speaks of the body as a denying source (please not too much, not all the time!) "As soon as all three-brained beings of our Megalocosmos acquire any self-awareness, they begin consciously or instinctively to dream of going to that holy planet, in order later to have the happiness to become a particle of that Greatness, the blending with which must sooner or later be the lot of every essence; and three-brained beings who have attained greater self-awareness eagerly and even joyfully permit unpleasantnesses from privations to their planetary body . . . They carry on a relentless struggle against the wishes of their planetary bodies, so that there should be formed from this 'Disputekrialnian-friction' those sacred crystallizations from which their higher Divine being-part arises and is perfected". (shortened)

"You need a good knowledge of the body for this work", says mind, misquoting from Kathryn Hulme's book, p 94 where G really said: "Very important that you know the body ***as a whole,*** for this work".

* * * * * * *

10th December.

More afterthoughts on knowledge of the body. Ouspensky talked of imagination in instictive centre, body protesting against things that are harmless, even healthy, like eating greens. There is an obligation to keep well if you can, an aim to know how much your body can and can't stand.

One chanced to re-read a passage about breathing exercises in ***Fragments***. It has always been a puzzle. There are warnings against artificial breathing which may put out of action the power to breath naturally, and there is "over-breathing", too much oxygen is harmful as well as too little; and yet there are references to breathing as if there were some useful secret about it.

One can guess at the possibility, if the habit were there, of controlling, say, anger by diverting attention to the ribs and inhalation for a few breaths as a sort of stop; or of breathing with a feeling that the air is connecting you with the great world, pneuma, spirit; one has only had the briefest experiences of anything like that. There is the story of the burning sigh of the man who was late for prayers at the Mosque.

But a cold in the nose has just been a breathing exercise of an involuntary sort, saying "life depends on breath", as Mr. B made us understand after his night watch through one of Mrs. B's crises. For this body-led person the chief lesson of a fast day was the importance of food. Without a next meal to look forward to, time seemed endless; though it can hang just as heavily for other reasons too, after lunch for instance.

Beelzebub's remarks (chapter ***America*** p 957), on the digestive disturbance from the clock change in crossing the Atlantic by sea, were prophetic. The greater disturbance to daily rhythms by air travel is now well known, and the rhythms have acquired a name "Circadian" which admits them to science.

We cannot Declare Independence of air, food or sleep for long. While we are alive we depend on the body and the body depends on Nature. It is just because life without a body, its powers and memories – "disembodied spirit" is a sad expression – is so unthinkable, that one is thankful for the idea of a finer, immortal body laid down, organ for organ, in the physical body by work and suffering.

Look up the Mathnawi story of the sigh in Mr. Bennett's war-time selection of extracts, "*Values*". Oh dear, here is another chariot, in the Maitri-Upanishad. How much further is the trail going to lead? Are these two section never going to be finished?

This chariot is much the same as the one in the Katha-Upanishad and is possibly of similar date, which it is maintained must be A.D. and not B.C., because they show signs of knowing of events connected with the origin of Christianity, although the theory is too vague to be made public. It was a little old volume given by Mme Heliane, "Oriental Poems" by Sir Edwin Arnold, selected by J. M. Watkins, 1904, which made one guess what the sacrifice of Nachiketas and his dialogue with Death might represent. These Upanishads would not be the only scriptures claimed to be a good deal older than they probably were, leaving their date and authorship to be guessed at.

* * * * * * *

What can't be cured must be endured. "If we accept our suffering without resentment or complaint we are, according to Gurdjieff, either paying off an old debt or laying up future merit", said Orage, quoted by C. S. Nott in ***'Teachings of Gurdjieff: The Journal of a Pupil'*** 1961 "If we pass on our suffering to others, it becomes 'evil'." "The saints are eaters of suffering."

If in a moment of waking up we can cut hurt pride or self-pity out of a suffering, it is a form of transmutation or intentional suffering. Maybe it will be useful later, be good for brain hygiene or do some soul etching. Though one could never be aware of it at the time, looking back over the years one may feel one must have benefited from repeated work, though the old enemies are still there when vigilance isn't.

This work doesn't need miraculous powers, only honest self-observation and repeated practice, and the help of a good deal of carrot and stick from outside – both encouragement, and pressure to fight against. There must have been a foundation of right education by teaching and example. How fortunate one is to have had that, and then to have met, through J. G. Bennett and Ouspensky, the unsystematic Gurdjieff "system" which instinct said "cling to at all costs", though it didn't square with an academic training.

A week before his death Orage told Nott: "You know, I thank God every day of my life that I met Gurdjieff". This is in the biographical note in "Alfred Richard Orage: ***Essays and Aphorisms***", Janus Press. Orage's dates were 1873 – 1934, so he was probably a few years older than Gurdjieff.

Perhaps one form of "first conscious shock", preparation for transmutation, is arguing it out against mechanical thoughts; the process acquired a name from this passage about "active reasoning with oneself" – "Well, Merslukin called me a fool. But why should I feel hurt? Actually for me personally, I am not hurt – not because I have no pride or self-love, perhaps I have more than any of you; but perhaps it is my pride that does not allow me to feel insulted . . . . I reason about it . . . . If he called me a fool, does it follow that he is wise? . . . . I know that in this case I am not a fool, so I am not offended. On the other hand I may have been a fool. In this case I should thank him for letting me see that I behaved like a fool. I shall think about it and perhaps not act foolishly next time." This splendid talk by Gurdjieff about active reasoning and about true and false pride and the impossibility of distinguishing them in oneself, is in C.S. Nott, p 51 and in "***Views from the Real World***" p 274, given at the Prieuré, February 13th 1923. In the latter self-love only is used; pride does convey more in English and was perhaps added by Orage.

One thing which rather confirms that Gurdjieff had Plutarch's dialogue on the Moon in mind when he wrote his chapter on Purgatory is that both give unorthodox, if different, theories of re-incarnation. Plutarch makes Psyche and Nous rise towards the moon at the first death. For Gurdjieff Earth is only a remote and minor, if particularly unfortunate, planet in the vastly enlarged universe of modern astronomy; so at the first sacred Rascooarno of beings, wherever arisen, in whom second and third bodies have been coated, these "rise both together to that sphere where those cosmic substances – from the localisation of which the body-Kesdjan of a being arises – have their place of concentration". (p 765).

In Plutarch, after the second death, when the Nous, Mind, has gone to the sun, the Psyche should gently dissolve back into the moon, but a restless ambitious Psyche may try to return to earth. It is no slight or harmonious business if a psyche without a mind manages to seize a new earthly body. It is a possible way of explaining a Typhon, a Hasnamuss or a Hitler.

G uses his myth to convey emotional urgency for effort, speaking of the objective terror felt by higher-being-bodies, which have arisen but not reached the degree of Reason (Nirvana?) able to exist without a Kesdjan body and not be subject to any external "painful" influences, when their Kesdjan body dies, as it must after a certain time. Then such still unperfected higher-being-parts must seek another Kesdjan body just vacated. This is a reincarnation in "the sphere just mentioned", not a return to the familier earth. (pp 766, 768).

When their Reason was perfected to the required degree the higher-being-bodies were in the beginning taken on to the Most Most Holy Sun Absolute, but after a terrifying and unforeseen common-cosmic misfortune the sacred Theomertmalogos, food of higher-being-bodies, issued changed from the Sun Absolute, and higher-being-bodies were coated with "sins-of-the-body-of-the-soul" in their presences (p. 799). Then the beautiful planet Purgatory was set aside, where the higher being parts could do the intense work of purifying themselves. This planet is outwardly paradise but inwardly hell, constant anguish for the souls who have fallen there after inexpressible, consciously suffering labours, and who see OUR COMMON FATHER ENDLESSNESS HIMSELF so near and so often but are still unable to help him on account of the undesirable elements present in them.

* * * * * * *

21st November, 1974

Could one, without an enormous hunt, find that Greek philosopher who taught of something like a Sun Absolute? After an interval comes a faint memory. Isn't it in ''the book of centuries'', a notebook of dates arranged on a plan learned from the P.N.E.U. – not Pneuma (breath, spirit) but Parents' National Educational Union? Yes, it is there, the philosopher was Philolaus. Still one had to spend another exceptionally rainy day rereading various articles, mostly P's, with Philology as a diversion beside Philosophy, and making no progress.

Greek philosophy did not start in Greece but in what is now Turkey. Koestler calls the Ionian philosophers of Miletus ''polite atheists''. The earliest, Thales, 640–546 B.C., who learned geometry in Egypt and successfully predicted an eclipse, said the primary matter was water; Anaximenes c. 590–525 said it was air. Persian conquest drove some philosophers into exile; Xenophanes of Kolophon, north of Ephesus, started the school of the Eleatics in S. Italy. He attacked the anthropomorphic scheme of gods of Homer and Hesiod. The Eleatics said ''All is One and One is God''. One and Many is a favourite philosophical distinction.

Ephesus was the home of Heraclitus, c. 540 – 475, the ''Dark Philosopher'' who emphasised change, ''everything flows'', and said fire was the primary substance. He used the word ''Logos'' as reason or order in the visible world.

Empedocles of Agrigentum (Sicily), c. 490 – 430 B.C., greatly revered by the townsfolk, is stated to have first said there were ***four*** ultimate elements, united and parted by two forces, love and strife. The four elements fire, air, water, earth, became part of the stock-in-trade of philosophers and physicians for the next two millenia. Now we have plasma, gas, liquid, and solid, but a hundred or so elements. Plutarch's "On the Control of Anger" quotes with approval a saying of Empedocles, "Fast from evil".

Another line does link with Athens. Pherekydes of Syros (one of the Kyklades islands in the Aegean), also said to have studied in Egypt, belonged to the circle of Peisistratus (605? – 527 B.C.), the successful tyrant of Athens, who had the Homeric poems collected for public recitation. Pherekydes founded an Orphic community and is credited with first teaching metempsychosis and the immortality of the soul. He was one of the teachers of Pythagoras.

Pythagoras (c. 570 – 500 B.C.) came from the island of Samos, off Turkey, and may have left because of the tyrant Polycrates, about whom Herodotus (died 425 B.C.) told the story of the ring and fish to illustrate that if a man is too lucky it is likely to end badly for him. A mixture of success and failure is safer, thought Pharaoh Amasis, who broke off his alliance on hearing how the sacrificed ring Polycrates threw into the sea on his advice was found in a gift fish which was opened in the kitchen. Amasis was proved right when Polycrates was lured to the mainland by a promise of gold and murdered, and his body hung on a cross.

After his travels Pythagoras settled at Croton in the toe of Italy, where his brotherhood became "something between a cloister and a college", prototype probably of the medieval universities of Europe. His is a famous name, often met; he is an intriguing but somehow elusive figure. How mysterious it is that a new birth of ideas was happening at much the same time in such widely separated parts of the old world, with Buddha, Zarathustra, Confucius, Lao Tse, Orphism, Pythagoras. Metempsychosis or transmigration, defined as the passing of the soul of human beings or animals at death into a new body of the same or different species, vegetarianism, self-denial, contemplation, are Pythagorean doctrines which remind one of India.

What should the name Pythagoras mean? Snake in the market place? Prophet in the market place? Agora, located in the dictionary under agora-phobia, means assembly or market place: Python: great snake killed by Apollo at Pytho (Delphi);

also a familiar spirit, in New Testament Greek. Pythia, the oracle priestess at Delphi.

The Pythagoreans found irrational numbers ''arrhetos'', unspeakable, a word that reappears in Jung. Irrational numbers (not the same as imaginary numbers) seem to be ''non-terminating decimals'' like $\sqrt{2}$, the diagonal of a square with sides of one unit.

Now Philolaus. He is the chief name among the successors of Pythagoras and was born in S. Italy about 480 B.C. He took refuge at Grecian Thebes when the brotherhood was persecuted and the meeting houses burned; two of his pupils at Thebes were later present at the death of Socrates in 399 B.C. Philolaus was able to return to Tarentum (on the heel of Italy) which was the headquarters of the later Pythagoreans. ''As a philosophic school the Pythagoreans became extinct about the middle of the 4th century'', (i.e. around 350 B.C. for someone who will confuse 4th century with 400's and still makes mistakes counting backwards for B.C.) There are Pythagoreans and Neo-Pythagoreans in the last century B.C. and first century A.D.; one would much like to know whether some brotherhoods were continuous with the early ones.

Though Pherekydes left a cosmogonic treatise, Pythagoras only taught orally. Philolaus was the first to publish a book on the Pythagorean doctrines and this book was used by Plato for the Timaeus. What did publication involve in those days? The introduction to the Penguin Herodotus says that in his time, the Greeks possessed no books, they heard them read at private gatherings or public festivals. When books had to be copied by hand the importance of libraries, such as that at Alexandria, is evident. The ruins of the Qumran community on the Dead Sea show that, like the monks later, the Essenes were copiers of books.

Pythagoras is credited with discovering that the earth was a sphere and not the flat disk or cylinder of the Milesians, but Philolaus is supposed to be the first who said the earth moved and was not the centre of the Cosmos (although later systems put the earth back in the centre). Philolaus postulated a Central Fire, also called the Hearth of the Universe, House of Zeus and

Mother of the Gods, round which revolved the spheres of the earth, the moon, the sun and the five planets, with the sphere of the fixed stars outside all. A counter earth was added, Aristotle says, to bring the revolving spheres up to the sacred number 10, or else to help explain eclipses. It appears as if the earth revolved round the central fire once every 24 hours, our side always turned away from it and from the counter earth, as the moon keeps its other face always turned away from us. Philolaus supposed the sun to be a disk of glass which reflects the light of the Universe, as in Gurdjieff's chapter ***The Arch Absurd,*** where our sun neither lights nor heats but is in reality covered with ice.

Some say Pythagoras discovered the five perfect solids. Philolaus connected them with Empedocles' four elements, the tetrahedron with fire, octahedron air, icosahedron water, cube earth. The fifth, the pentagon-dodecahedron, was either aether or the universe; perhaps its 12 faces could suggest the 12 houses of the zodiac. Why isn't a sphere a perfect solid? How did the ancients manage without paper for making models? Papyrus? The perfect solids and their ramifications have fascinated many people through the ages and have even been pursued into higher (Euclidian) dimensions. Even if one cannot go so far, their study is perhaps good for the brain. Koestler writes about the astronomer Kepler (1571 – 1630), who had a kind of vision connecting the ratios of the Copernican orbits of the planets with the five perfect solids, that it was "one of the rare recorded instances of ***false inspiration,*** a supreme hoax of the Socratic daimon which speaks with such infallible intuitive certainty". But it was in pursuit of this idea that Kepler came to his real discoveries about the orbits being slightly elliptical, using the observations and measurements of the Danish astronomer Tycho Brahe.

Democritus of Abdera in Thrace, contemporary of Socrates, studied seven years in Egypt and worked out a mechanical system of atoms; soul-atoms were round, smooth, specially mobile, like fire atoms, and intercalated between body atoms.

About the great Plato let us only borrow another quotation from

Koestler's ***Sleepwalkers*** (Penguin 1959), ''As so often with Plato, it is impossible to say whether all this is to be taken literally, or allegorically, or as an esoteric leg-pull''. You might call him a legominist. One feels this applies to Plato's statements about women, and about homosexuality which was to become so prominent in literature, but one remains puzzled.

The Athenian philosophers from Anaxagoras (about 500–428 B.C.) through to Plato and Aristotle used the word Nous as Mind, Intelligence or Thought acting in a world of ideas, forms or patterns, separate from this visible world. Idea comes from a root id, to see, and logos from lego, speak. Although ''forms'' convey nothing, the concept of two worlds, of another world located not so much ''outside the sphere of the fixed stars'' as interpenetrating the visible cosmos, ''in the air'' but imperceptible to our senses, surely makes it easier to express the possibility of divine rule and of life after death. Helen Waddell says the Desert Fathers gave the world the idea of Eternity, for the sake of which their legendary austerity was worth while. It is the same two-worlds theme with richer content.

''You can't really leave out Socrates'', the model, who submitted to the death penalty by hemlock when 70 years old, – but how to do justice to him? At least pick a few points from Professor A. E. Taylor's article. Socrates is immortalised by Plato, but Aristophanes, Xenophon and other writers also testify to him. The Periclean age witnessed one of the ''bankruptcies of science'' (as students are turning away from science now). Cosmological speculation had led to a chaos of conflicting systems each only able to prove its rivals wrong. Socrates turned the interest of philosophy from cosmology to ethics. His message from God was that the great business of life is the ''tendance'' (therapeia) or care of the soul. After Socrates' time psyche means what soul means to us (does it?) ''the normal waking personality, the seat of character and intelligence''. (Having scorned ''dead languages'' at school, belatedly one sees the point of a classical education and wishes one had it, but there may be some advantages in being an amateur.)

Socrates' character: ugly, short and stout, he had a keen

sense of humour, called irony by his opponents. "Though the purity of Socrates is beyond question, he really had an ardent and amorous temperament". Despite his endurance, self-imposed hardship and poverty, he was no self-tormenting ascetic and he could be the soul of merriment at a gay party. Summer and winter his coat was the same; he had neither shoes nor shirt.

Stopped in mid-Socrates; surely one read "he never took money for his teaching" (so no wonder he was poor), but it can't be found anywhere. Next day it was better to give the philosophers a rest; some days were turned towards the transmutation paragraphs till again bogged down, in waffle about energies which are too complicated.

Yes, the bit on philosophers is nothing but a precis of the encyclopaedia, done with the formatory or formulating apparatus; but plod on, maybe we need them.

Here is another line, Diogenes and the Cynics; one had not registered before that they were connected back to Socrates too. Antisthenes, c. 444 – 365 B.C., pupil or friend of Socrates (who is said at the end of his life to have repudiated the idea of disciples), taught that disrepute and poverty are advantages in the pursuit of virtue. He attracted the poorer classes by his simplicity of life and teaching. His cloak, staff and wallet became the uniform of the school.

Diogenes was born at Sinope in N. Turkey about 412 B.C. and died in 323, reputedly on the same day as Alexander the Great. He was a pupil of Antisthenes in Athens and soon outdid his master. He did not live in the famous tub, belonging to the temple of Cybele, all his long life, for on a voyage he was captured by pirates and sold as a slave. He spent the rest of his life in Corinth, tutoring his master's two sons and preaching self-control. At his death the Corinthians honoured him with a statue of a dog. (Cynic, kynikos – dog-like).

Putting away the Diogenes volume the echo flashed, Sinope – sinapi, mustard. Is this another far-fetched explanation of the mustard seed parable? The dictionary had once accidentally yielded the information sinapism – mustard plaster, giving the Greek for mustard; could the parable be explained by some play on words? Diogenes and the Cynics could represent a Western tradition of asceticism and self-denial, which after all is a trend liable to appear and to be exaggerated, as one pole in any preaching of ethics.

An illustration from J.M. Barrie's Peter Pan leaped to mind, Mr. Darling sleeping in the dog-kennel in evening dress in penance for his children's disappearance. Perhaps Diogenes was the model.

In unbroken succession down to the time of Hadrian the Cynic school was represented by men of strong individuality, if tactless, but it also attracted charlatans. Epictetus warned a young pupil of the difficulty of being a true Cynic: "Cast about for a dainty dung-heap whereon to have thy fever". The Cynic "must show that plain and simple open-air living are not mischievous even to the body". Diogenes "went about radiant with health and with his very body he turned many to good".

In Mark chapter 7, Jesus sent out the twelve in pairs, with ascetic instructions to take nothing for their journey save a staff only, no scrip, no bread, no money in their purse, shod with sandals and not putting on two coats. In Matthew chapter 10, and Luke chapter 9, they are not even allowed staves. The sending out of the seventy in Luke chapter 10 with similar instructions is peculiar to this gospel. Seventy is a number associated with Egypt because of the Septuagint (Latin for seventy) or Greek Version of the Old Testament made there.

The Cynics lead through to the most famous school of later antiquity, the Stoics, thus connecting them too with Socrates. There are two Zeno's. The one who founded Stoicism is given slightly varying dates belonging to the first generation after Alexander's conquests; 336 –264 B.C. are one set. He came from the Phoenician city of Citium in Cyprus and visited all the schools in Athens, attaching himself chiefly to the Cynics for their practical character. When he started to lecture it was in the Stoa, a frescoed colonnade beside the market place in Athens. (Could it be the ancestor of medieval colonnaded cloisters?). The Stoic system spread widely in the "Hellenistic" world, the countries into which the successors of Alexander carved up his conquests. Tarsus, Rhodes and Alexandria became the chief Stoic university centres. The independent Greek city-states had disappeared; the Stoics preached cosmopolitanism, the common brotherhood of all men and races.

Logos was an important word with the Stoics, taken over from the Cynics, but they extended it throughout the natural world, (an influence from Heraclitus) as an active force interpenetrating passive matter. Gurdjieff's teaching that everything is material (of varying fine-ness) might have been drawn from the Stoics.

Zeno's own writings have not survived, but he is said to have declared images, temples, sacrifices, prayers and worship to be of no avail. A really acceptable prayer can only have reference to a virtuous and devout mind; God is best worshipped in the shrine of the heart by the desire to know and obey him. Why, it is close to a favourite text, ''Go ye and learn what that meaneth, I will have mercy and not sacrifice'' (Mathew 9.13: also in chapter 12). The original is in Hosea. I Samuel 15.22 says: ''To obey is better than sacrifice, and to hearken than the fat of rams''.

Democritus, Empedocles, the Sophists and the Cynics had looked for deeper meanings in the old myths, but Zeno carried allegorical interpretation much further. If the surface meaning of an old story is repugnant, look deeper. Elaborate allegorical explanations such as those by Philo of Alexandria, or by Maurice Nicoll in ''The New Man'', give the idea of not taking stories literally, which may lead to seeing simpler symbolisms in them for oneself; but myths should remain puzzling as ''the Unconcious'' remains puzzling. Though sex symbolisms do run all through mythology, to dismiss it as nothing but that is to miss the point. ''A symbol can never be taken in a final and definite meaning'' (*In Search* p. 283).

In *Every Good Man is Free* Philo quotes a saying of Zeno: ''Sooner will you sink an inflated bladder than compel any virtuous man to do against his will anything that he does not wish''. This could be a more meaningful connection for Gurdjieff's bourdiouks.

* * * * * * *

9. *Prayers?*

12th December 1974. "Man's worst invention ever was the football shirt.... any distinctions by which he divides all people up into the 'goodies': our team who wear our shirt and the 'baddies', the opposing teams who wear a different shirt and whom he is free to hate, damage, speak evil of and often kill". "With what motivational instruction do we replace the largely displaced religious ethic?" (Motivational instruction is called education for the feelings, the horse.) "We have to replace the teaching of loyalty to nation, class, ethnic group, tribe or religion by teaching the very broad idea of loyalty to mankind". Meredith Thring in ***Machines – masters or slaves of man?*** Publisher: Peter Peregrinus.

The striking, almost inspired, image of the football shirt was a factor in provoking this writing. One **is** deeply imbued with the idea that one "ought" to love all humanity, sympathise with the poor, subscribe to feed the starving on the Indian sub-continent, that equality is an absolute value; but it is all incomplete.

Those who cry for more for the low-paid, the handicapped, the pensioners or the "developing countries", at the expense of taxes on industry and national insurance stamps, not of their own personal sacrifice, are often hypocritical, doing it as propoganda for political effect, or they are lazy thinkers. Help which encourages population growth only increases future poverty.

Love for all humanity is rather vague; maybe loyalty, like charity, should be begin at home, but not end there. It would mean renouncing the usual method of cementing group loyalty by hatred of outsiders.

There is an opposite mood which sees "humanity in the mass" as the enemy before whom pearls must not be cast, from whom one must escape to a higher level, trying to preserve and hand on the pearls to the few who can respond. Then humanity is seen as apparently determined on self-destruction like the Garadene swine. Ouspensky wrote of Russian suicidal tendencies inevitably leading to the revolution and the death of old Russia. All these irreversible changes kill something. Now the suicidal tendencies seem to have appeared in almost every country in the news.

The word "selfishness" has been avoided because it smacks of school homilies and because some selfishness is necessary; you must safeguard you own basic needs, and know what is good for yourself before you can know what is good for others – but plain selfishness, unashamed self-interest is rampant, and must lead to general breakdown.

Can state socialism, or anarchy, or affluence either, do away with the failings of human nature? Corruption, power-seeking and violence reappear, increased by insecurity or the loss of ethical inhibitions. Sometimes one does believe in the doctrine of original sin, a built-in stupidity.

Both pro and anti-humanity moods are automatic. Where one senses such a contradiction it is a sign that neither view is sufficient; that from the clash of affirming and denying one needs to wake up, to force up the level of consciousness in the hope of further understanding.

Humanism is sometimes only an anti-religion shirt, but at its best it is a fine ideal. It can be extended to include care of man's habitat earth, and possibly to include the dead, though its tendency is to look to the future of the race in time rather than the future of the individual in eternity. All the same it is not reasonable to think man was put on earth just to please himself, or that he is the highest being there is,

Thring speaks of the "to a young child incomprehensible problem of loving an intangible invisible God". One's own experience has rather been that four and five years olds sometimes bring out surprisingly clear thoughts about God. The doubts and difficulties come later or are present in parents and teachers who feel they cannot give the traditional instruction sincerely. This feeling is one motive for trying to explore these questions more fully in this writing. Education is failing if it does not give material for the discussion. In one's own school days there was an impatience, why don't they teach us the things we really want to know? Not so easy, one sees now.

It must be from childhood churchgoing that the writer acquired an ingrained idea of the Almightyness of God. So sometimes she is angry with that God because he does cruel things. Gurdjieff avoids the problem of how God can be both omnipotent and kind by making our ENDLESSNESS, or his chief assistants, fallible. The earth's misfortunes are due to miscalculation or unforeseeingness. And even the Sun Absolute is subject to Time, the Merciless Heropass, and in danger of gradual decay. Memory says H. G. Wells' Mr. Britling solved the problem by saying God himself was subject to Necessity, to Law. Or one can say having made the rules God abides by them, unlike elder brothers who change the rules to suit themselves as the game proceeds. "Even God sometimes does not have enough attention to go round", Mr. G is reported to have said.

Marx told the Socialists history would inevitably bring them victory. Christians too have thought they were on the winning side, God must win in the end. It is good for "morale". But what really counts is to be able to keep going when your side looks like losing, and when the battle is in the balance, as Churchill, the old bull-dog, was able to put heart into us by his broadcasts during the years of Dunkirk, retreat and blitz.

Gurdjieff is able to present our ENDLESSNESS as a Father sorrowing over his foolish children. Beelzebub's plan for educating his grandson, like Gurdjieff's in his teaching, was to tell his stories without giving his own opinion, or to assert absurd, contradictory opinions, so that Hassein should form his own convictions out of conflicting experiences and questionings. It could be said we are not to take our God ready-made but to form our own ideal, find our own conscience, and so build our being, and this is one reason why God disguises himself and allows apparent evil to flourish.

In earlier days Mr. Bennett gave members of his groups the task of writing him a monthly letter, and very subjective they probably were, but a post-script after-thought remains as true, that what the writer needed more than anything was to find God. Probably she had a wrong idea of God and she certainly did not know where to look for him. Now – and it must be thanks to Gurdjieff – she has found a conviction that there is intelligence and power there behind the invisible curtain, a someone or some many concerned with our affairs. She hesitates to call it God. Those who say God is darkness, unknowable, unexplainable, are the best theologians. The conviction is not always there but it can be re-argued when its absence is felt.

One may maintain God is so wonderful he can care directly for every one of the myriad individuals, or one may feel it is more respectful and realistic to say our affairs are in the care of lesser members of a hierarchy. Europeans have been conditioned into believing in the absolute superiority of monotheism, but is even that so necessarily certain? It probably started by analogy from Pharaoh or a ''King of Kings''. Still one does want to believe that the same God can be present in London, Calcutta or Timbuktu. Ordinary thinking should not pronounce on theology, but it will try. Contradictory aspects may both express something useful.

At the time of the contact with Gurdjieff there was a feeling that you could really trust him to know what he was doing and to be acting for the best – or if you couldn't, then you could trust no one at all, so it was worth putting your stake on him, like Pascal betting that God is. If the bet is right you are saved; if it is not, there is no hope anywhere else either, so there is nothing to lose.

Coming back to loyalties, subsidiary groupings may be seen as ***limbs or organs*** of ''all humanity'' or ''organic life on earth'', if individual men and animals are cells of a great Being; but it feels right that the gospels should present love of neighbour or of humanity as the ***subsidiary*** law, with love of God or of the ideal of love itself as the primary law.

''Verily a husband is not dear, that you may love the husband, but that you may love the Self through the husband, therefore a husband is dear,'' says the Brihadaranyaka Upanishad, in ''Bible of the World''. The fomula is repeated for wife, sons, wealth, Brahman-class, Kshatriya-class, the Worlds, the Devas, creatures; ''that you may love the Self through everything, therefore everything is dear''. The note says this ''Self'' is not the egotistic or individual personal self, nor soul, but the Universal

Soul or Self which is in each of us; perhaps the nearest is "God within us". (Can you find him?). The Great SELF, I AM, Person, of which all our separate selves are cut-off parts, is an appealing conception of God, and makes every self matter, be of concern to God, to whom it wants to return.

It is hard to find precise meanings for philosophical words, but the Upanishad expresses the feeling one has about loving for love's sake, not just when the object is attractive. As the speaker says to Maitreyi, "Let me make a settlement between thee and that Katyayani, my other wife", so one tried to connect it with the Maitri Upanishad. Perhaps they were written in the same school.

At seventeen the writer, being depressed lodging alone in an ugly Paris suburb in 1931 after five months in the fairy-tale South German Schloss, determined one night to pray until an answer came. Nothing happened, she only got cold and sleepy and had to creep into bed. Yet there was really a kind of answer, it was meeting the Gurdjieff system, with its Paris connection, seven years later. Now she would be inclined to see the incident as "planned" for her education, perhaps even carried out by her dead mother, Dorothy.

The morning and evening prayer-saying soon lapsed without much guilt in the rush of life at college; it was only vain repetition. A small lesson about prayer had happened more than once in school days – the loss of a protractor, dearly-beloved six-inch ruler. After a good search the thought would come, "You've done what you can, now you can ask 'Please God let me find it'." After that it would soon turn up, perhaps shut into the atlas. But this prayer wouldn't work now. Now she says, "Own up, where have you hidden it?" and has to wait till lost things are pleased to reappear, though she still hunts. Spectacle case must be found!

The nursery formula repeated kneeling by parent at good-night time, "God bless Mummie and Daddy and Meddie and Janie and make B a good girl" comes back as worthwhile, but could one teach it to children oneself? Blessed is a lovely word though one cannot say quite what it means.

Socrates said prayer should just be ''Give me what is good'', for we don't know what is good for us. Verbal prayers often sound designed to put an idea across to the congregation rather than seriously addressing a deity. Even Father Christmas cannot grant all requests.

Good behaviour is a prayer, to earn help, to try to be worthy of getting what you want. Begonia, Beg on Jah, pray.

* * * * * * *

15th December 1974

Received news yesterday afternoon of Mr. Bennett's death at 77 on Friday 13th December. Had been reading yesterday morning Institute circulars strangely posted with no envelope, ''Closing Sale'' of the Journal ''Systematics'' after eleven years, and proposals for yet another grandiose project, a community in USA based on 418 acres and self-sufficiency, which was reminiscent of the early post-war venture in S. Africa. At that time Mr. Bennett had an old book on the history of various communities in USA, rousing questions of why some, usually religious, succeed and last many generations, while others soon break up.

Tikliamish: apart from Takla Makan and fancies about tickling friends, the only association found and remembered is whether it could refer to the Amish, a small American sect who ''stopped the clock'', will not use electricity or motor cars, keep their old-fashioned costumes, hymns of 1571 and tunes never printed. To fill some time, read them up again, via Spinoza's friends the Collegiants, to Mennonites, a group of sects taking their name from Menno Simons 1492 – 1559, a Dutch priest repelled by the excesses of the Munster Anabaptists (re-baptisers). Menno left writings, celebrated the Lord's Supper with feet washing, rejected the Trinity as not in Scripture and prohibited marriage with outsiders. The Amish, with some 8,000 members in the 1920's, are a sect on the conservative side of the group.

''Take a wife from thine own people'' seemed in general to be good advice, but the story of Ezra making Jews who had married strange wives put them away is so unfeeling that it calls up the contrary story of Alexander compelling his soldiers to take Persian wives.

Could Gurdjieff possibly have been thinking of the Amish? The history of heresies is intriguing just because one wants to understand what drives them. G might have been interested in sects because of the question how his own work was to be preserved without losing too much quality; he shows the danger by his teaching of octaves, that in all spheres of human activity, lines of development deviate and even turn into their own opposites. (*In Search* p 129) Amish hymns are mentioned in the encyclopaedia, and the Moravian brethren were known for their singing; G provided music and "temple dancing" rather than singing. Many sects have been based on Bible reading and/or on books by their own founder; books evidently are a means of speaking direct to future generations. G did write books and keeping these alive, so they do not get lost in the flood, may be one task for his groups.

On the other hand sects may also be a warning, against fossilising a teacher's legacy. One admires the way Kathryn Hulme took what Gurdjieff gave her out into the world and made something good out of her war-time job as a welder on Liberty ships, in the harrowing work for displaced Poles, and then by her books, without belonging to any group.

16th December, Memorial Service. John Godolphin Bennett, "Mr. B" or later just "Mister" – we owe him, in one way, everything, for introducing us to the Work, leading us for years, continuing and broadening our education; but in these experiences he has played the role of 'enemy', to be avoided because his magnetism would overwhelm the small pole of own inner judgement. Even so dual may be our relation to "God"?

* * * * * * *

18th December. Is there anything useful one can say about bringing up children and how it turned out, after years of informal child-minding? There was a theory and a hope, long since lost in the welter, that if you kept watch on your own inner state, something might rub off into them.

Feelings from one's own childhood provided some starting-out points: if possible never lie to them, pretend to know more than you do, or to be right if you made a mistake; to have a reason for orders, if it's only "or I shall get tired and cross", but "because I say so" was not allowed; to encourage hand work, collect scrap wood, nails and paper, provide tools, sewing cards, weaving; to have apparatus for games, dressing up clothes, home-made swords, bows, shields, helmets, cloaks, paper crowns, old tins hammered unscratchy, for drums, shops, mudpies; the top hat of a real clown. Two battered wooden guns were made as leaving presents by Ben and Mark grown past playing themselves.

But the usefulness of tidy habits and good manners, the encouraging of interest in reading or arithmetic, or more important, of truth-telling, not stealing, gentleness to smaller children, girls and animals, temper control, respect for sex, that swearing is a bad habit, that life can't be all easy – where these were needed there has been no success in inculcating them. The action has been the other way round, the children's games and quarrels, their sayings, their impulsive coming and going have been guidance *to* this "deputy mother", or "tormented governess" fretting lest the furniture get broken.

29th December – 1st January 1975. News from Sherborne, Mr. Bennett's "Academy", now in its fourth year. Wondering about the shape of the future and writing "It is really a time to 'pray' for guidance", one comes against the question ,"Is the future fore-ordained, can we influence it either for better or for worse?"

Long ago Mr. Bennett was giving a talk at Coombe Springs and looked up at the ceiling then covered with (fake) stepped parallel beams, copied from a Florentine room. He said something like "there are parallel lines of time; on the higher levels there are more breaks in the flow of deterministic causality, which people on those levels can fill in freely".

A different analogy was found in a copy of his first book, ***The Crisis in Human Affairs,*** on whose jacket the words printed in red had been left out. Could it not be that freedom was only a chance to fill in the right missing words, not any words one liked?

One must not push the analogies too hard, the question of free will is beyond logical thinking. In discussing the future "fore-ordained", "planned", "mechanically determined" are not the same. In 1947 we had little conception of action by "Higher Powers".

An analogy for "their" planning is seen in housekeeping over the Christmas period; make sure there are enough supplies in the house for the many days of shut shops but the detailed menu can be worked out as you go along. Whether getting caught out by an unforeseen new Bank Holiday on January 1st contributes to the analogy, or only to admitting it to the writing in "revenge" for the emotional disturbance, is uncertain!

Perhaps the responsibility we do have towards the future is to keep channels open, to be on the watch to find our role in an impromptu drama. We might miss our cue and spoil the plan or it would have to be altered to work without us.

30th December. This writer feels she must have benefited from several years of Mr. Gurdjieff's "movements", mainly taught by Mr. Bennett. The first class felt like "coming into a birth-right", something missing since the gymnastics and folk dancing of school days; but she was shocked to realise in later years that the lessons of attention were not being carried over into posture and action in everyday life. She has not much experience of "meditation type" exercises, though there were Mr. Bennett's 1,000 daily "topics" given in 1946 – 1949. She feels there is a danger of putting too much faith in exercises or other methods; they are a means, not a salvation in themselves. Conscience, discrimination of what to do at this moment is what has to be found – just now, get up and dressed!

31st December. At another Coombe meeting: "How is it men and women don't destroy one another?" Mr. B. "They do destroy unless they create". Subud having R.C. type views on birth control, that couple went on to create six children in this over-crowded world. Now father has retired with three children still at school; but they have made a good family life.

10. *An Example of Mental Functioning: ''Heaven's Doorstep''*

22.4.74. Some words were in the mind on waking: ''looking for its reward in changed lives'' – ''a few'' – ''but is a few enough?''. While meat for the cat's breakfast was cut up, someone's criticism of the Flying Saucer fable was repeating itself. ''(Children respond more to moral ideas presented indirectly) than as rules or obvious morals''..... ''You could describe the actual arrival in heaven'' ....While its owner was dressing single sentences began composing themselves in this uninventive head. Stop and write that one down. Later they must be put in order.

PARABLE

At school Garry was rough and a bully and showed off by swearing and talking big instead of learning. He cheated, and got out of trouble by blaming other people if he could. As he grew up he was proud of his strength and good looks; but he never did a thing for anyone else. He thought he was impressing the girls, but he did not stick to one, so when he got fat and less handsome they just found him a nuisance. He didn't bother to visit his parents or help them when they were older. After they died there was no one who cared what happened to him.

As the birthdays went by he grew old and sick in his turn. He grumbled and complained and looked miserable; people didn't like him for he made them feel miserable too. He got older and weaker and finally he died.

He found himself on a dry stony waste, littered with rubbish, plastic wrappings, beer cans, broken glass, He had shrivelled down to six inches high; there was something wrong with his left foot, he stumbled and had to crawl. He was hungry and thirsty; he tried to chew the spiny cactus but it was too tough.

He climbed a big stone and saw some people and angels that seemed to him a long way off. He dragged himself towards them. He called but no one heard. At last he was near enough to tug at the ankle of one.

"Why don't you help me?"

"You never cared for anyone but yourself. Now its too late, no one wants to help you."

However, finally the angel, who had once been his mother, and still cared, picked him up and put him in her pocket with his head out. He watched while other new arrivals were welcomed and escorted to live with their friends and relations; the finest ones joined the angels to help in their work.

At last the shrivelled dwarf began to cry. "No one told me. It's not my fault I was selfish."

"Oh yes they did. They told you at school."

Presently the dwarf was really sorry; he remembered people who had been good to him and his heart began to melt. His twisted foot got a bit straighter.

"Isn't there anything I can do to be useful?"

"Well", said the angel, "You can stay here by heaven's doorstep and keep it swept clean. If you do that well, you'll begin to grow again."

The doorstep seemed very big and so did the broom, but he struggled with it and began his new job. People going in took no notice of the little creature by the doorstep, but now he didn't mind, his service was useful and some day he would be allowed in. He slept in a tiny porter's lodge and food was provided.

Sometimes he did feel lazy or sulky or angry, and he would kick the hard stone; but then he saw his foot turning in again, and his hands shrivelling and wrinkling, so he made himself go on with his task. Every Christmas he measured himself against marks on the doorpost – a tiny bit taller. As he got quicker at sweeping, he used his spare time collecting some of the rubbish into piles and it was taken away; but more kept appearing from earth people's thoughtlessness.

It took him a thousand years to grow back to man-size in a fine straight body. Then one happy day a big crowd of angels came to welcome him into heaven.

* * * * * * *

Various contributory threads could be traced. There had been a "payment", an emotional shock the afternoon before: Andrew climbed the temporary fence at the bottom of the garden and was seen to be crying. Better go and play mother. "Those boys have taken my bike and thrown the key in the rose bush". Go round with him to the stony waste where a motor works has just been demolished; shock, suppose the boys refuse to give up the bike. Mercifully they don't.

Street sweeping here is a three-day operation because notices "No Parking – Street Cleaning" have to be left 24 hours on alternate gutters; and at once fresh litter is thrown down.

An image of our own doorstep beyond the corner of the room presented itself as the ideas came. Someone had recently said he wanted to be useful, not reach some hypothetical higher state. "You ought to start with the (dwarf's) earthly life." "Can't handle that" – then begin to see how. "What about food and sleep?"

At first one was elated after writing it out; by evening, as often, reaction set in, "Silly – all day long to sweep one doorstep – it must be holy-stoned". The story set out to be a warning and turned into one of second chance.

It was noticed that items presented themselves and were accepted more because they were probable, yet there was no attempt to think what the symbol meant or whether it was appropriate. Ideas were borrowed, principally from a favourite story in which rich man stood on tip-toe for 1,000 years to look through a peep-hole into heaven. It is in "Dreams by French Firesides" sent home by a German, Richard Leander during the siege of Paris, December 1870 – January 1871, translated and published by A. & C. Black in 1890, illustrated by Louis Wain.

Further, the processes – outside stimuli, different states of the brain, unexpected discoveries or fittings together – by which the whole of this writing has grown, are a study in mental functioning so confusing that it is held to imply the work is being planned from "somewhere else". What is to be done with it remains to be seen. A reader may complain of lack of plan and consequtive argument. A patchwork it is. If the sentences won't behave, let's break the rules deliberately; better not make it too much of a habit though.

Mrs. Marsh, Mr. Gurdjieff's German translator, told us she asked him why he wrote in cafés instead of on the beautiful terrace at the Prieuré and he explained, ''I fill my heart with love for these people and from this I write''. This person seems to take a daily dose of fear of revolution by reading the newspaper, and to work from that.

11. Stop Press: Late News

Onion – union. To illustrate how the puns belong to a different part of the brain, not abstract-logical: it was only while working in the vegetable patch and talking to herself about inability to grow spring onions that the writer realised this early and obvious pun had not been included. Go and make a note of it at once. The recollection of puns and spellings by such associations has gone on for over a year. (A mistake, this one *is* in the earlier list but the incident is typical.)

Mosquito. ''I had been thinking about work. My little son was crying in the night from mosquito bites, I beat him. I was so horrified I would not let myself sleep again that night.'' ''I am very glad. This has shown you. Sometimes it happens like this when a person wants to work; sometimes Higher Powers even send the mosquito. Your little son is your teacher now and I charge you with a commission for him, five candies a day for a year.'' This is taken from notes of the reading at Colet Gardens of a Paris meeting report, so it is not verbally accurate, but ''sometimes they even send the mosquito,'' originally such a surprise, became a seed – or egg idea.

Roses. Draft a sentence with three ''so's'' in it. The tendency to repetition persists and sometimes eliminating one only produces another. Has Mr. Gurdjieff's standard caution to an enthusiastic new arrival, with its inverted echo of ''on the third day he rose again'', still not been included? ''First day: roses, roses: next day: so, so, so. Third day, thorns, thorns.''

* * * * * * *

Plan	–	Napoleon, Laban
Verb	–	(word, logos) brief, birth, phurba (Tibetan magic dagger) ver, worm. Biafra. St. Briavel's. Hermann von Baravalle (Rudolf Steiner geometer)
Black	–	Cybele (why can't we have K not C in Greek names?) black hole, club
Bubastis	–	beast, paste, pest, bust, stop, step

The similarity lavatory – laboratory was a childhood start for "spelling". School jokes, whether dirty or just verbal tricks, and the puns of Beryl the Peril and Dennis the Menace, have more point than one realised.

Bog is Russian for God so the name Bogachevsky in ***Remarkable Men*** got the fanciful meaning "God will achieve, complete the psyche" and Pogossian, which sounded like Bogassian when read aloud, Bog assis ane, the Lord seated on a donkey, the entry into Jerusalem.

Obligatory – Bog lie at ory.

More puns and symbols:

Salad – Mr. Gurdjieff's delicious chopped salads had so many ingredients, almost "a bit of everything in the world". They are an excuse for making this writing such a hotch-potch, a zig-zag patchwork. It is not for speed reading.

Mr. G's "small secret", the offer to pay in dollars, which secured him a prompt Citroën when there was a long waiting list, could suggest paying by dolours.

Fridge – Phrygia (from Greek phruges – freemen), a varying central region of Turkey or Anatolia (Greek sunrise, or Eastern land) – The Phrygians were northern immigrants of the second millenium B.C. but they could not displace the "original Asianic" Great Mother religion. On the contrary the worship of Cybele spread into Greece in the 5th century B.C. and was established in Rome in 204 B.C., whence it reached even the Rhineland and Britain, so perhaps following the earlier route of the agricultural Megalithic culture, which also had a Great Mother theme. One reads that even earlier the hunting people had a "Lady of the Beasts".

Wellington boots – well linked on (united)
Hero – Here O
Detergent – deter – gent, keep men off
Pears – pairs, couples
Yoghourt – (girt) enceinte
Brussels sprouts – Common Market
Crab – cancer, carbuncle
Wood, woodwork – the cross, preparing the cross, one's own?
Hexagon – Hexe (witch) and agon can always be agony
Starlings – Australians (also Ernest Starling, author of Principles of Human Physiology, Mother's stepfather)
Coathangers – Sydney bridge
Children's building blocks – bricks to build a new world, brick by brick (*A & E* p 1184)
Continent on the map – alas the incontinence of old age; may one pray to die before reaching that stage? also continent, chaste
Maxwell – make swell, pregnant – it can be of an idea
Embroidery on huckaback (towels) – Commentary on Habbakuk (Dead Sea Scrolls)
Needle-book – a book about needing God (El)
Rabbit – Rabbi, Rabboni
Ammonia – Ammon Jah (the Egyptian God Amon)
Diamond – die amand, die loving, rather like "Blessed are the dead who die in the Lord"
Apron (just washed one) – chastity, or birth control, protection
Change of life, menopause – a warning of death

Picked up the antique saucer by its rim: the modern cup (czechoslovakian) was too heavy, the rim broke. Rim was supposed to suggest Mir, Russian for world.

A father fond of puns asked about the S.S. Themistocles, in which his wife and small children came "home" from Melbourne, Australia, in 1919, "Where is the Mrs. Cles?" A swollen left toe joint, afflicting both him and his daughter, is held to suggest Croton and Pythagoras.

One has read that 17th century thinkers hoped by encouraging scientific investigation to divert interest from the disastrous religious quarrels. Now one has a small hope that interest in the mind's relation with the unconscious might divert some attention from politican quarrels, though too much interest in the unconscious is probably quite as dangerous as too much science.

Here is someone cheerfully doing his best in a not too easy situation. Preaching to such as he would be out of place but some refreshing novelty, a few jokes, may be heartening.

12. An

The gospels and Acts echo with names in An – Anna, Annas, Antioch, three men called Ananias. In Semitic languages words like Anuki, ana, ani, mean "I". Perhaps they do all derive from the Sumerian sky god An or Anu; his daughter was Inanna or Ininni; we hear also of Oannes (a name for the water god Ea or Enki, teacher of civilisation) which suggests the name John with its many forms; and of an Egyptian fish An. Annaeus was the family name of Seneca, Nero's tutor, his brother Gallio (in Acts) and his nephew Lucan.

The syllable associates many words, annual, anus, ane, anneau (ring), botany, animus, animal, analogy, psycho-analysis (ana – up, luo – loose), Ani the town (*R.M.* p 87). A.N. Whitehead, sister Anne on the roof in Bluebeard, anonymous, ancestors, Leonardo's beautiful St. Anne smiling mysteriously behind the Madonna, till one would like to spell 'Unconscious' An-conscious and think of Anna as a kind of goddess of children's play, feeding them ideas, for they seldom run dry. But she is also a goddess of power, with a sinister side, Durga, Kali the dark mother with a necklace of skulls, that the living should fear death. Remembering death a silence falls on the inner busyness, a vacuum that cannot be sustained long, time standing still, a kind of prayer, a gap through which something may come later. It dams the stream of activity to raise the potential energy.

To get some meaning out of one too-early death, the name was twisted to "spell" "Guard (the) Tart An", as if the Unconscious was a whore, who had to receive all that was put into her. Maybe she does have to receive all the grudges and hates and results of cruelty – bad karma – and this is why she causes so much mental illness. For the personal unconscious to be wholesome, and insulated from real harm, so that it can be awakened without insanity, and the rational mind losing control altogether, mental cleanliness and hygiene would seem to be safeguards. This "woman" should remain under tutelage of the "male", the conscious reason which must keep the function of criticism and ethical responsibility, so that the unconscious does not run wild.

Is not this why we are enjoined to hunger and thirst after righteousness, to be poor in spirit and peacemakers – the eight beatitudes; or to follow the Buddhist noble eightfold path, Rightness of view, aspiration, speech, doing, livelihood, effort, mindfulness and rapture? By cleaning up inside you can help outside, and tune your receiving set.

An educated conscience would seem to go beyond following rules of conduct to discriminating what is needed in this specific moment for playing our role in the theatre of life. Some things Mr. G did may not be for imitating; we cannot know all the circumstances. He stressed remorse of conscience. If remorse is used as a force for work in general, or to redeem the consquences, the original mistake can be turned to good.

"Blessed are they which are persecuted for righteousness' sake: for theirs is the kingdom of heaven," says the eighth beatitude. Does this kind of payment absorb, neutralise, redeem some of the world's ugliness, by the transfer of merits? Is it like Gurdjieff's intentional suffering? But how many of us can face that, in spite of sometimes "being our own worst enemies" or 'having a tendency to masochism"? An easier interpretation is that the intention is God's, not ours.

* * * * * * *

IV

RIDDLES

1. Supporting Quotations

Some extracts follow which are relevant to the themes of this book.

Sir Oliver Lodge's definition of Spiritualism: "the name.... is more usually employed to signify a growing persuasion on the part of certain people that the activity of human beings is not entirely limited to the use they make of their bodily or material organisms on this planet. It is held that those organisms were constructed by an animating principle which having entered into relation with matter for the purpose of developing an individuality can continue long after the temporary material body is worn out or otherwise resolved into its elements; and, further, that the personalities thus brought into existence shall carry with them their memory, character, tastes and affection, which they had developed here while in association with matter, and shall be able under certain limitations to guide and influence terrestrial affairs in co-operation with those still living on the earth". (Encyclopaedia Britannica)

Socrates: "No one knows with regard to death whether it is not really the greatest blessing that can happen to a man". (Plato, Apology, "Last Days of Socrates", Penguin, p. 60).

From ***"Aurelia"*** by Gerard de Nerval (G. Labrunie) 1808 – 1855 translated by Geoffrey Wagner 1958:
Visions during insanity IV. "One evening I was positive I had been removed to the banks of the Rhine. In front of me were sinister rocks, their silhouettes dimly outlined in the gloom. I went into a cheerful house, where a ray from the setting sun cut through the green shutters which were festooned with vines. It appeared to me that I was entering a house I knew well, belonging to one of my mother's uncles, a Flemish painter who had

been dead for more than a century . . .

I lay down on a four-poster bed . . . In front of me, hung on the wall, was a rustic clock and on this clock was a bird which began to talk like a human being. I had the idea that my grandfather's soul was in that bird . . . .

I saw an old man tilling the earth. I recognised him as the man who had spoken to me through the bird's voice, and, either because he told me directly or because I understood it innately, it became clear to me that our ancestors take the forms of certain animals in order to visit us on earth . . . .

I understood . . . .that in this world I was now visiting the ghosts of material objects accompanied those of human bodies.

I entered a large room where a crowd of people had gathered. On all sides I found faces I knew. The features of dead relations, whom I had mourned, were there reproduced in others who, clad in more ancient costumes, gave me the same paternal greeting.

'Then it's true,' I exclaimed delightedly, 'that we are immortal and retain here the replicas of the world we once inhabited. What happiness to think that everything we've loved will always exist around us! I was very tired of life'

'Don't be too quick to rejoice,' (my uncle) said 'for you still belong to the world above and you have still to undergo hard years of trial. The abode that so delights you has itself its sorrows, its struggles and its dangers. The earth on which we lived is still the theatre where our destinies are woven and unravelled. We are the gleams of that central fire which gives it life and which is already growing weak . . . .'

'What!' I cried, 'Do you mean the earth could die and we be hurled into oblivion?'

'Oblivion,' he answered, 'does not exist in the sense it is understood, but the earth itself is a material body whose soul is the sum of the souls it contains. Matter can no more perish than mind, but it can be modified according to good and evil. Our past and future are intimately connected. We live in our race and our race lives in us''.

III. ''Many times the idea has occurred to me that in certain serious moments of life some spirit of the outer world becomes suddenly embodied in the form of an ordinary person, and influences or tries to influence us without the individual in question having any knowledge of it or remembering anything about it.''

Aurelia was the name of a visitor to Coombe Springs, Dutch housewife with a neurosis – an urge to go up and touch people for reassurance – which started from a night of terror in the Nazi occupation. One has a superstition about the influences of names; in this case the discovery of Nerval's Aurelia was years later.

From *''Philip in Two Worlds''* by Alice Gilbert (Andrew Dakers Ltd 1948). She believed these to be telepathic messages from her Merchant Navy son after he died in a pedal cycle accident in August 1945:

September 4th 1945. ''They have given me a message for you – let yourself drift...'' ''What do you mean by they?'' ''All of them – there's all grandpa's pals. I'm a bit confused, but it seems as if there are all his brothers and sisters. I did get your aunt F. – imagine – young, gay, and busy composing music! We can't drag her away from it – sits at the piano all the time.'' ''How, a piano?''

''It's a thought creation of grandpa's – such as you used to speak of – he managed it. He seems to be their leader and helper.''

September 13th

''So many people here don't seem to be alive in my sense.... I see so many people who never seem to try to use their new powers to get anywhere. They just stay round where they've always lived.... It does seem to me that people on earth badly need education for death – not so much 'religious', as common sense instruction on how to make the most of their opportunities.''

September 14th

''My new body does not need food in your sense; it is nourished they tell me, by magnetic currents emanating from the source of Power. That is why anyone given over entirely to the Powers of Negation must eventually disintegrate, because they automatically 'cut off supplies', in a way of speaking.''

September 29th
"You are much helped by the tough determination shown by most of your relatives here. They are just as obstinate and strong-willed here as they were on earth. What they want, they go all out for! Those people seem to do better here in the long run, even if they make mistakes."

October 4th
"The longer I stay here, the more I realise there is no 'magic' or unlimited power in the post-death state. We have simply changed the form of our 'incarnation' .... But it is infinitely freer than the physical body because we are now directly using our thought force as a means of transit and linkage. If a person's thought force is deficient, diffused or undeveloped when he dies – then it is just too bad! His activities are limited in proportion, but, if his life has been reasonably honest and 'up striving' in the sense that he has not been too grossly material and selfish, then it seems he can attract more developed people, who do try to help him along."

October 9th
"...it is hatred and cruelty which are the really unpopular sins, in the eyes of Higher Plane people."

October 11th
" – Do dogs come over after death? – Some do... The great majority of animals re-incarnate over and over again in a sort of group – that is the cause of 'instinct', which so intrigues zoologists."

October 12th
"There was a group of little boys who had died in concentration camps. They are still in their child-form, for their spirits had newly emerged, and are undeveloped by any earth experience, but they rapidly become entities here with a little help. At present, they are still frightened, and think they are hungry because fear and pain had been so deeply impressed on them in life that their etheric bodies were affected as well as their physical. I managed to create a football for them, and showed them how to play it, in a sort of skimming way; they responded

quickly, and are now laughing and gay because they have forgotten."

Whilst the sincerity of the accounts of Alice Gilbert, Edgar Cayce, or "The Boy and the Brothers"(Swami Omananda Puri, Gollancz 1959) is convincing, one does not necessarily take the theosophical, reincarnationist or Platonic cast of the revelations at its face value. It could be that "the spirits" are not giving away their secrets but using some convenient existing system of ideas; or it could be a sign that Western ways of thinking need some corrective which oriental thought can give.

"Novalis" 1772 – 1801.
"Alles, was wir Zufall nennen, ist von Gott." (Tagebuch, 27th July 1800) Everything we call chance is from God.

Arthur Koestler ***"Arrow in the Blue"*** p244. He speaks of his bridge-burning impulse to join the Communist party, (which probably saved him from the gas chamber), when he had a fine job on a Berlin newspaper. It was the result of series of catastrophies on a December evening in 1931; he woke next morning with a super hangover mixed with self-reproach, anxiety and guilt, next to a person he disliked, financially broke from gambling at poker, and with a bust up car.

"Now I have always held a perhaps superstitious but deep belief in the significance of events which come in series. When major and minor calamities crowd together in a short span of time, they seem to express a symbolic warning, as if some mute power were tugging at your sleeve. It is then up to you to decipher the meaning of the inchoate message .... the warning may have been issued by that 'he in me who is more than myself'. Later on I discovered that André Malraux holds a similar superstition – or belief; he calls that tugging at the sleeve by apparent coincidence 'le langage du destin.'

In my opinion, the 'language of destiny' is often couched in vulgar slang."

Here may be mentioned Edgar Wallace's surprising law, "if you hear a new word for the first time you will hear it again within

24 hours''. One did not realise that detective fiction had an esoteric element.

There is also the saying ''Breakages come in threes''. In personal experience they have often come in twos; after that one took fright and handled the china more carefully.

Granville-Barker, 3 plays, 1909 – ''Waste'' p 324: ''God is infinitely economical and wastes perhaps less of the power in us after our death than men do while we live.''

It is suggested this is the double meaning of literary misers such as Molière's or Balzac's.

Max Weber. Speeches in Munich 1918
. . . . (how a power said to be both) ''omnipotent and kind could have created such an irrational world of undeserved suffering, unpunished injustice, and hopeless stupidity. Either this power is not omnipotent or not kind, or entirely different principles of compensation and reward govern our life, principles we may interpret metaphysically, or even principles that forever escape our comprehension.''

''Ideas come when we do not expect them and not when we are brooding and searching at our desks. Yet ideas would certainly not come to mind had we not brooded at our desks and searched for answers with passionate devotion.''
from Max Weber, selected and translated by Gerth and C.W. Mills, Routledge 1948.

An outsider's view: Ananda Coomaraswamy. ''Transformation of Nature in Art''. 1943 p 159. ***Use of Images in India.*** ''Again, wheras we are apt to suppose that the religious significance of Christianity stands or falls with the actual historicity of Jesus, we find an Indian commentator (Nilakantha) saying of the Krishna Lila, believed historical by most Hindus, that the narration is not the real point, that this is not an historical event, but is based upon eternal truths, on the actual relation of the soul to God, and that the events take place, not in the outer world but in the heart of man. Here we are in a world inaccessible to higher criticism, neither of superstition on the one hand, nor of cynicism on the other. It has been more than once pointed out that the position of Christianity could well be strengthened by a similar emancipation from the historical point of view, as was to a large extent actually the case with the schoolmen.''

Elsewhere he says that religious intolerance is practically unknown in India, (though a breach of social etiquette may involve excommunication from society).

Another oriental view, (source lost) ''What the Christians tell you to do is excellent, what they tell you to believe is absurd.''
(Krishnamurti, in Rom Landau's ***God is my Adventure***, 1935. p349.
I am, however, against all ***authority*** in spiritual matters....''
P 359. ''Religions offer people authority in place of truth, they give them crutches instead of making their legs strong; they give them drugs instead of urging them to push out along their own paths in search of truth for themselves. I fear none of the churches today has very much to do with truth.''
Suzuki, in Eranos Yearbooks, 1954
A footnote: ''Is it not a somewhat futile effort on the part of the Christian theologian to try to prove the historicity of Christ and then to proceed to tell us that for this reason we must believe in him?''

''That philosophy is not at all conducive to one's spiritual welfare may be seen in Kierkegaard's parable of the palatial mansion built by the philosopher, (but he lives in a hovel next door).'' Footnote: ''But as long as we are human beings given to the habit of intellectualising, philosophy is inevitable, I believe. For one thing it is entertaining anyway.''

Alan Watts, ***The Legacy of Asia and Western Man – The Middle Way*** 1937 p 69. ''Christianity seems to be deficient in religious technique. It is too much inclined to offer supposed historical facts as a means of salvation. (The church should emphasise) the Christ story as an inner experience for each man, he is to be born in each one.''

St. Francois de Sales (near Annecy) 1567 – 1622. Letter to Mme de Chantal, 24th June 1604.
''....les convulsions de l'enfantement spirituel ne sont pas

moindres que celles du corporel."

Arthur Conan Doyle (in a foreword to Violet Tweedale, ***Phantoms of the Dawn,*** 1924)
"My own information on which I may not at present enlarge, is that a great period of chastening trial awaits humanity, and that when this has passed it will be shown that what we have done in our day and generation was to familiarise the world with those ideas, which were to be the seeds of the universal simple undogmatic and practical religion of the millenial future."

If only it were possible! It would have to allow for the whole range of human experience and of the earth's history, and how can you speak of experiences you haven't had? It seems there will never be a millenium, and multiplicity, conflict and mystery are necessary. Organisations can seldom keep their quality for long before a new reform is needed, but books and works of art do speak direct to successive generations.

Belstead School prayer sheets.
"Habit is a good servant but a bad master."
"By taking thought you can build any habit you choose to build,"

Hilaire Belloc (Daily Telegraph book review, 17th October 1974).
"Oh, let us never, never doubt
What nobody is sure about."

* * * * * * *

2. July 1974. Tapes
Release more tapes – the Watergate clamour?

When a "rabbit", whose instinct was to hide, was forced to take courage and ask Mr. G for an interview in August 1949, he said, "Tomorrow eighty – a hundred people wish to see me" – typical exaggeration. Then a change of tone, "Understand this heat for me very trying, today I nothing interior have." How could one press him? Yet thanks to Elizabeth the interview took place, in the little inner store-room which others had described. "Sorry you go. I not eat so well now you go."

The question, pinpointed by Mr. B, must be brought out.

"Mr. Gurdjieff, I am always so tired". "You wish to know whether you have illness or not?" He would give pills, not for cure, just for observation. Take one a day, do any exercise, count to 100, just to help absorption, keep journal; when the pills were finished, write to him.

There was one last lunch. Rabbit was on tenterhooks about getting the pills. Suddenly he looked up and spoke to someone who fetched a tube of twenty Roche Vitamin C pills. "You see, I promised," he said. In shame over the fears the rabbit got a fit of conventional manners; "Thank you Mr. Gurdjieff." "Thank you is nothing. Or not thank now, maybe later when you find zeroes in cheque book."

The rabbit went home clinging through a stormy seasick night crossing to a glimmer of hope, the clue he had given, which was really just "observe, keep journal". It seemed to say "trust your own careful observation more than what anyone else says."

This one brief personal contact is not much qualification for writing about him, in comparison with those who knew him for years; but there was a feeling that one could meet him also through his books, he had put his best into them.

There was a parallel and contrast with an earlier single interview. Shortly before the war, on a work Sunday at Lyne, this then green recruit was led without warning through the beautiful reception rooms for an interview with Mr. Ouspensky. She was too shy and unprepared to be able to think of anything to ask, so the opportunity was wasted, but some memory of it was imprinted.

At the end of February 1954 an emotional shock turned the rabbit's world upside-down and it seemed an invisible world really did rule our affairs. Living in a dream-bubble or Yezidi circle, not to be stepped out of without punishment, in a state of concealed insanity, her head was full of whirling ideas and imaginary experiences. After some months came an idea "Has it been Mr. G helping us?"

Early on, when the mind was in a wild state, it got what was considered to be a revelation about the story of Gurdjieff's birth in the ***Arousing of Thought*** (*A & E* p8), when the sound of an Edison phonograph poured through a hole in the window pane made by their crazy lame goat and the midwife had in her mouth a lozenge saturated with cocaine of German make. Lame ''crazed'' or rearranged is an anagram for male. (Goat Capricorn is G's birth sign.) Edison – Dei Son, Son of God. Cocaine German lozenge: Nicea Co(uncil) Z – last (last letter) Nolege – Knowledge Manger; i.e. that after the Council of Nicaea the esoteric understanding of the birth of Christ disappeared.

Esoteric comes from the comparative of eso – within but soter means saviour; the Greeks liked puns. The idea of esotericism is present in the Gospels. ''Unto you it is given to know the mystery of the kingdom of God: but unto them which are without, all these things are done in parables.'' Mark 4.11. There is a mountain, a ladder or stairway to be ascended; but contrast Matthew 11.25 ''thou hast hid these things from the wise and prudent, and hast revealed them unto babes.''

Our father used to say that Christianity was spoiled when it became the State religion. He hated what he called priestcraft, and once walked out of the church when the Athanasian creed, with its endless definitions of the Trinity, was to be sung. The idea, that some secret tradition about the origin of Christianity has been lost, did stimulate curiosity, leading to interest in the history and writers of the first century A. D. Gradually one got to know one Roman emperor from another, thanks in the first place to Robert Graves' Claudius books in Penguin.

* * * * * * *

Sunday 26th May 1974

Looked up Confucius, he prized the Yi-King or I-Ching, Book of Changes, used for divination with yarrow stalks.

Next morning recalled a review about Danish bog burials, which mentioned a wreath of yarrow. Why yarrow, it always seemed such an uninteresting little plant? Ah, but those flat composite heads, all joined to one stalk underneath – it is like us in the visible world, or islands in the ocean, joined via the sea-bed.

Let's look it up. On the way, pass ''tansy'' at the head of a page. Another herb, let's read it. Gosh, athanasia does mean immortality, a-thanotos, not-death. The herb name comes via medieval Latin and the old French tanesie. Is that the real point of the Athanasian creed, the creed of deathlessness?

Anastasia means standing again, resurrection, which is startling in view of the controversy about the survival of Anastasia when the last Czar and the rest of his family were shot.

* * * * * * *

Another "revelation" was about Joseph Smith, 1805 – 1844, who claimed to have unearthed, in obedience to a vision, the golden plates on which the book of Mormon was written. These were supposed to have suggested the golden plates recording the postures for the priestess-dancers at the Sarmoung monastery in G's *Remarkable Men* (p 162). The stormy early history of the Mormons, like the Anabaptists and other sects, is something of a caution against easily accepting "revelations" or guidance from "the Holy Spirit" or the unconscious. G's account of the training of the dancers as young girls is like what one reads about the training of Indian temple dancers, who were also temple prostitutes; but it is also like the training of Russian ballet dancers in its precision and exactitude of performance. Could one of G's "monasteries" be the Army Medical School in St. Petersburg?

Thanks be to an Aunt Annie whose legacy was her copy of the Encyclopaedia Britannica, the fourteenth edition reissued for the coronation of George VI, 1937. Looking for something else one came upon Bekhterev, Russian neuropathologist 1857 – 1927, almost as famous as Pavlov it seems. In 1893 he became Professor of the Military Medical Academy in St. Petersburg and was elected director in 1905 – 6. He founded in 1907 an institute to foster psycho-physiological research. One of his books was called "***The Functions of the Nervous Centres***", 1909.

A mind always looking for secret connections jumped to the conclusion that G might have based his early psychology on "centres" as a tribute to Bekhterev. At least in ***Remarkable Men*** he does twice mention reading absorbing books on neuropathology. (p 63, p 70).

Koestler says that Bekhterev published a book on "*Biological Radio*" in 1916. "*PSI, Psychic Discoveries behind the Iron Curtain*" (1970 paperback, Abacus) describles his work on animal telepathy with a famous circus trainer Durov, published in 1920. Bekhterev went on to study telepathy in humans, and the physiologist Dr. Leonid Vasiliev (died 1966) from the Bekhterev Brain Institute, was a leading Russian E.S.P. researcher under Stalin and again in the 1960's.

* * * * * * *

Another queer idea was that the map of pre-sand Egypt (**R.M.** p 99 and p 120) stood for the pre-Georges Sand state of "the literary secret". On the basis of the small selection of books one chanced to read about that time, one had formed an over-simple theory that there was a literary secret rather as Koestler describes in his autobiography "*Arrow in the Blue*" (written about 1951). He was born in Budapest in 1905. When he was 13, having just read Othello, Koestler said to a professor,' "But what I don't understand is the hidden meaning.... well, *you* know that there is only one kind of secret.' I had as yet no notion of sex. But I had an absolute, unshakable conviction that there was a basic central mystery, related to eternity and the infinite, and that some fraction of the secret was contained in all great works of literature, and in fact their greatness and fame were due to their containing part of the mystery" (p 37).

John Ruskin wrote in "*Sesame and Lilies*", ... if the author is worth anything.... you will not get at his meaning all at once, – nay.... at his whole meaning you will not for a long time arrive in anywise. Not that he does not say what he means, and in strong words too; but he cannot say it all; and what is more strange, will not, but in a hidden way and in parables, in order that he may be sure you want it."

The Armenian priest in whose house G copied the map was thought to be Jean Jacques Rousseau (1712 – 1778) because a portrait of Rousseau in Armenian costume was found reproduced in an old school prize. Now another look at the Rousseau article, a good one. Why, here is something new that rings a bell: "he became, or says he became, secretary to a Greek archimandrite who was travelling in Switzerland to collect subscriptions for the rebuilding of the Holy Sepulchre." G has an archmandrite travelling with a miraculous ikon to collect money for Greek relief (*R.M.* p 81); a special service to pray for rain was held before the ikon, and rain came. Perhaps the "Holy Sepulchre" is still being rebuilt.

The writer of the article evidently considers Rousseau's "Confessions" a bit too tall; you might say his stories are intentional inexactitudes, though wonderfully vivid and concrete. One feels the same about Cellini's autobiography and De Quincey's "Confessions of an English Opium-eater", and indeed about Josephus' adventures in Galilee. G's proposed book "The Opiumists" (footnote *A & E* p 917) was thought to point to De Quincey.

"There is little doubt that for the last 10 or 15 years of his life Rousseau was not wholly sane....These Confessions were written, if not under hallucination, at any rate in circumstances entitling the self-condemned criminal to the benefit of considerable doubt." Discussing Rousseau's great influence for the next 100 years, the article says "part at least of his literary secret was the common property of almost everyone who attempted literature." (Mme de Warens 'spells' Nazareth)

A friend, Sydney Jenkins, said Lubovedsky meant Love of Truth. It is difficult to be sure what made one think G's Prince Yuri Lubovedsky, who also copied the map of pre-sand Egypt, might be Count Leo Tolstoy (1828 – 1910). Tolstoy did say Rousseau had tremendous influence on his student years. Prince Yuri went through a time of apathy and disillusionment (*R.M.* p 155) which might point to the despair preceding Tolstoy's conversion in the later 1870's.

Reading ***War and Peace*** with enthusiasm during the 1939 – 1945 war, one was puzzled that the philosophy of the wise old Russian general, who just let things happen, should be so like the dictum "Man cannot do" in G's "system" as taught by Ouspensky. It was only years later that one realised G might have taken it from Tolstoy.

Tolstoy's new religion never gained many disciples but his

general influence was world wide. He attacked the artificial life of the rich, and compulsion by the state, preaching non-violence. He disapproved of revolutionary activity because it breeds hatred and more violence.

In ''*What is Art?*'', Tolstoy's new standards led him ''to reject or to minimise by far the greater part of modern art and literature.'' Gurdjieff too was scathing in his rejection of ''subjective art''. The responsibility of the artist is a big question.

Like a number of other men worthy of admiration, Tolstoy apparently found it necessary to deny immortality. It seems impossible such a man did not experience intimations of immortality, though it may have been desirable to oppose the various doctrines of people who too easily asserted they knew all about it without question. William James in ''***The Varieties of Religious Experience***'' (p 184) takes Tolstoy and Bunyan as examples of inner unification, but says ''it is hard to follow these windings of the hearts of others, and one feels that their words do not reveal their total secret''. These were Gifford lectures at Edinburgh in 1901 – 2, so Tolstoy was still living. His end was dramatic. The tensions with his wife and family built up so much that he left home on October 28th, 1910, with his youngest daughter Alexandra. He was taken ill at Astapovo and was laid up in the station-master's room, dying on November 8th(21st). His Anna Karenina had suicided under a train.

Railway lines can be a symbol for time, history. A dream of getting off a train preceded news of a death. A life like Tolstoy's is used to shape history, though we may not understand how.

A recurrent dream of escaping from some enemy by hauling oneself by a rope across vast Russian plains has not reappeared since the rope was identified as a railway track, memory of Intourist journeys by train Paris-Berlin-Warsaw-Leningrad-Moscow-Kiev and back in 1935. Great-aunt Ella had offered a choice between this or a repeat of earlier trips with her. There was a feeling of ''ought'' to give her the pleasure, but brother said ''Never mind ought, choose what you *want*''. There was no doubt Russia was the wanted choice, never regretted.

A re-reading of the Chapter ''***Professor Skridlov***'' brings up the detail (p 238) that Father Giovanni had been a slave. This suggests Epictetus, the Stoic sage, once a slave of Nero's favourite Epaphroditus, who did have him educated. When Domitian exiled the philosophers about A.D. 94, Epictetus settled in Nicopolis in West Greece, founded by Augustus to commemorate his victory at Actium. This must be the Nicopolis about which St. Paul had written to Titus (ch. 3 v. 12) that he had determined to winter there. Epictetus' "Discourses" were preserved by his pupil Arrian (about 96 – 130 A.D.) and the "Handbook" was adapted for Christian use.If Gurdjieff's toasts were drunk in water they were to sages instead of idiots.

3. *Tirade on Goodness*

Though passionately believing in the importance of goodness as a general direction of striving, and that we should indeed "hunger and thirst after righteousness" or "have a social conscience", this amateur writer has shirked defining goodness, because of the difficulty of excluding the "Pharisees" kind of self-righteousness and hypocrisy attacked in the gospels. "They say, and do not". (Matt. 23.3) "God, I thank thee that I am not as other men are". (Luke 18.11) In a talk in "***Fragments***" (p.156) Gurdjieff made a distinction between morality and conscience. Is not the work of conscience, of real discrimination about conduct, a work for soul-making or the work of a rightly formed soul?

We need as much as ever the basic laws of life in society, thou shalt do no murder, thou shalt not steal, thou shalt not bear false witness; but these are only a foundation.

What is a good apple? Ripe, juicy, free from rot: it is good for being eaten. So perhaps it is not goodness which should be defined but the aims or purposes behaviour is good *for.* A primary aim is to keep oneself alive and healthy and so things that are bad for the health are vices. Probably we do use the word "good" in different senses. "Good news" is not to do with virtue, though "Good, well done" may be, and in English there is some feeling that good is connected with God. Good is pleasing to God or to parents. Was not toilet-training the child's first meeting with the word?

"Be good, sweet maid, and let who will be clever." Often it is the less clever who become useful well-loved people by developing kindness and serviceableness, thus turning out cleverest in the long run. But can't the clever be good? Did we rate cleverness at school too high and underestimate goodness? Now the trendies don't seem to encourage either.

It is generally easier to say what is wrong with the world than to find solutions. Charity begins at home; maybe answers do too, doing one's own duty. "The best way of training the young is to train oneself at the same time; not to preach, but always to practice what you would preach", was already said by Plato in the "Laws". (729. Livingstone p 177)

For a general statement of aims or duties there are the five strivings (*A & E* p 386) in Gurdjieff's chapter on "***The Organisation for Man's Existence Created by the Very Saintly Ashiata Shiemash***" on the basis of objective conscience; or the definition of a remarkable man (***R.M.*** p 31) as one who stands out by "the resourcefulness of his mind, and who knows how to be restrained in the manifestations which proceed from his nature, at the same time conducting himself justly and tolerantly towards the weaknesses of others". Tolerance is a value fought for by our ancestors, which we are in danger of losing by tolerating those who would end tolerance if they got power. When does tolerance become permissiveness, complacency, laziness? Definitions cannot be all-embracing.

Here is someone who has managed to express something about goodness: Cicero "***On Friendship***" (translated by Michael Grant). His speaker Laelius has said friendship is only possible between good men. "Let us take some individual whose life and behaviour have displayed proven loyalty, honesty, fairness and generosity – a man of unflinching integrity. . . . someone whose character does not contain a trace of covetousness or violence or unscrupulousness. For such are the men who are generally described as 'good'." "Even when a friend is absent he is present all the same . . . . Even when he is dead, he is still alive. He is alive because his friends still cherish him, and remember him and long for him". (Penguin, pp. 186 and 189)

Men have been philosophising about ethics for thousands of years, how can you expect to sort it out? Must it really be read up? . . . . This is shorter: ''The Ethical Movement''. Ah, those posters one used to see on the Underground, the South Place Ethical Society. The movement was started in the 1870's by an American Jew training to be a Rabbi, '' . . .to advocate a religion of human fellowship and service, based upon the principle that the supreme aim of religion is the love of goodness, and that moral ideas and the moral life are independent of beliefs as to the ultimate nature of things and a life after death. . . ''

That is well put. This writing takes the opposite position, that in a world of increasing hatred and violence ''purely human and natural means'' are not enough to help men love the right, and that the care for the health of an immortal psyche is the most sensible kind of selfishness. It cannot be healthy unless it is ''clean'' towards its fellows, not ''in debt.''

In his myth about judgement, Plato says the judge may lay hands on the soul of the king of Persia or other potentate ''full of the prints and scars of perjuries and crimes with which his various acts have stained him, and he is all crooked with falsehood and imposture, and has no straightness, because he has lived without truth. . . .full of all deformity and disproportion, which is caused by licence and luxury and insolence and incontinence''. He is despatched to prison for the punishment he deserves. The curable ones are improved by the pain and suffering of punishment from their evil. The very bad men come from the class of those who have power; but good men, who fulfill their trust righteously, may appear in that class, and they deserve warm admiration. (From Gorgias, in Sir Richard Livingstone's ''Selections from Plato'', World's Classics. pp 209 – 211)

From the article on the history of Ethics one gathers that Socrates said virtue was wisdom or knowledge, involving the paradox that no man, knowing good, would do evil. This sounds like the source of the provocative dictum one feels one heard from Ouspensky: ''There is no such thing as conscious evil''. One admits that much evil does come from ignorance, short sight, stupidity and so one wishes to combat them. However.

in ***Fragments*** (p 158) it is put in less extreme form: "Nobody ever does anything deliberately in the interests of evil", but everyone has his own idea of what is good or desirable.

"The distinctive features of Christian ethics are obedience, unworldliness, benevolence, purity and humility", says the article. There is something in the criticism that the church wanted to encourage docility. Perhaps it was the battle with Gnosticism which led to the eclipsing of wisdom as a cardinal virtue (from cardo – hinge).

The Stoics had been moving towards recognising a duty of "rendering positive services to other men", but "definite changes introduced by Christianity" are:

1. Condemnation and finally suppression of the exposing of infants;
2. Abhorrence of gladiatorial fights;
3. Better treatment of slaves and encouragement of emancipation;
4. Much more provision for the sick and the poor.

Stuck in one's head is a story of a missionary in China who put up a notice by a pond: "Please do not drown unwanted babies here". Other cultures had ways of limiting population, and we rushed in to teach, without understanding the whole situation. It does illustrate the problem of doctrinaire application of a law, in this case "Thou shalt not kill" to all situations. We cannot go on Saving All the Children, it is only condemning them all to misery.

A primary problem of ethics seems to be how to induce people to forego an immediate "good" for the sake of a more remote one. It may be for their own future welfare, though smoking or drinking your health away is not entirely a private matter if some one has to nurse you. More difficult is to say why they should limit their own demands for what is good and desirable for themselves, for the sake of others or of the group. Our over-populated world is full of real conflicts of interest. On the smaller scale, one does not suppose it ever enters the thief's or mugger's head to consider the distress caused to his victim.

There are people one values particularly as good – reliable, upright, burden-bearing, loyal friends who will help in difficulties, fulfill duties – but there is an uncomfortable feeling that one cannot ask that everyone should be like that. It is one "form of will", one type, or kind of fate; and they and the world need other types too, more daring, restless, disturbing, or more creative.

Or would it be better to use the word "kind" instead of "good" when speaking of Will-types? One begins to see why Mr. Gurdjieff was elusive on the subject of type. If you feel your type is fixed, why make efforts? One thing that can be said is that being and understanding are not fixed, they can grow. This writer recalls struggling with – was it Jung's theory of types and their subdivisions, only to find he concluded that actual people are never exact types but individual combinations. Astrology does give a sense of the subtlety and complexity of type, will, fate and the way things happen, though there is something repellent both about fatalism and about the idea that you can manipulate fate just by consulting an astrologer.

Success and failure seem to be as much a matter of "luck" and guidance as of ability and work. You will go in the direction in which you have success. If you meet repeated failure you will try another direction. "Roses in one's outer world, thorns in one's inner", (K. Hulme pp 103 and 295) and vice versa.

One has a feeling that there is something wrong with preaching duties, or rather it does not go far enough. Evidently it must not become self-righteousness condemning others, or be just prigg-ishness and desire for approval as one discovered at school.

A theoretical answer was found while drafting the section on Purgatory and two stages of work. Carrying out duties, playing the role of the kind of person you want to be, is conscious labour. It is necessary but only the first stage. Then comes a failure, a mistake because you were not so conscious after all, an unnecessary sharpness or irritability from more giving out than you can afford – and a guilty feeling is nagging, imaginary "I" is hurt because it can't live up to its image. "Did you expect to be so perfect? Now see you are nothing, let all that go, and start again". One supposes this in the theory can be a form of second conscious shock. In an exceptionally dramatic moment the thought intrudes "Aren't you coping well, aren't you doing the right thing? (for once)" It does not mean one should stop trying to do the right thing, only turn away from the thought and bring attention back to the outer situation, which needs it.

Madame de Beausobré (Iulia Namier) once visited Coombe Springs. Her breakfast tray was taken in by someone who was probably wearing a frown, for Madame offered some advice: to have the right long term aims and be concerned in the immediate moment, but let the middle distance take care of itself, put away worries about the intermediate future. One listened to her with respect. Her book "***The Woman who could not die***" told of her imprisonment in Stalinist prisons and a labour camp. Amidst the cruelty of the system she sometimes also met striking kindness, mainly from the old camp doctor and other fellow prisoners.

Society seems to swing between permissiveness and severity. Puritan condemnation of theatre and dance, and the smashing of statues, make one think of Savonarola (1452 – 1498) and his "bonfires of vanities" and works of art; but his life seems to have been a kind of sacred tragedy. St. Francis of Assisi is perhaps history's most Jesus-like character, but Pasquale and Luigi Villari, authors of the article on Savonarola, evidently saw parallels with the gospels in his brief reign of popularity, trial instigated by the Pope, and method of execution.

How did Florence get to have perhaps more masterpieces per square mile than anywhere in the world? Because of, or in spite of, the turbulent history of the Republic? Or because of some racial inheritance from the ancient Etruscans? Cosimo de Medici, (1389 – 1464), of a banking family, "succeeded in dominating the republic while remaining nominally a private citizen", for thirty years. He was a great patron of artists and men of letters, and welcomed the Greek refugees from Constantinople.

His grandson Lorenzo the Magnificent was virtually a tyrant, but an able one who made Florence prosperous, and his palace was the school and resort of illustrious men. "His immorality was scandalous", but available sources do not report that he left any "natural" children, as was common in those days. He kept the pleasure-loving Florentines amused with masques and carnivals and wrote songs himself.

Lorenzo died in the year Columbus discovered America. He was only 44 and "his death cast a gloom over Italy". His unsuccessful son was turned out of Florence in 1494, leaving the government in chaos. Then Savonarola (soap-role, sorry!). The sensitive scholar became the fiery preacher, denouncing the sins of the world and the corruption of the Church. Prior of the Dominican convent of St. Mark where Fra Angelico painted the frescoes some fifty years earlier, was for a time unofficial and able ruler of Florence. When the crowd tired of austerities, his enemy the Borgia pope was able to bring about his imprisonment, torture and condemnation. He was degraded, hung on a cross with a disciple dangling from each end of the beam, and burned. He was a precursor of the Reformation.

As a youngster Michelangelo (1475 – 1564) heard his sermons regularly; it is said he studied Savonarola's writings with the Bible and that the St. Peter's Pietà, commissioned in 1498 "was as it were the monk's monument, created in his ecstatic spirit" (Ludwig Goldsheider, Michel Angelo's Paintings, Phaidon 1939).

4. *The Boolmarshano*

"In the opinion of Beelzebub, Man's Understanding of Justice Is for Him in the Objective Sense an Accursed Mirage". The chapter ***Justice*** describes how the Boolmarshano with the title "The Affirming and Denying Influences on Man" was made by Makary Kronbernkzion of the society Akhaldan on the continent Atlantis. One half of a copy incised on ivory reached an Aisorian priest near Lake Urmia where Beelzebub was able to make an alabaster copy of it; the other half he found in central Asia.

Mrs. Marsh, who made the German translation of Beelzebub, told us that she was sitting beside Mr. Gurdjieff when he was writing this chapter, so he took her name and the first syllable from a boulangerie opposite. Later an additional explanation presented itself; Boule – Greek for council, and Mars (Ares), for St. Paul's sermon about the Unknown God, on the Areopagus or Mar's hill at Athens.

Searching for anything which could correspond to the half of the Boolmarshano buried deep in Asia, one came on a version of St. Luke's prodigal son story in "The Lotus of the True Law". One of the speakers is the venerable Maha-Maudgalyayana which might be formed from Magdalen. One had an idea that Mahayana Buddhism received a vivifying influence from Christianity, as perhaps the stories of Krishna may also have done. It is interesting that the Nestorian Christians had spread right across Asia to China, and down into India, before they were decimated by the Mongolian conquests.

Sir Harry Luke in "An Eastern Chequerboard" (1934) summarises the history of the Nestorians, whom some call Assyrians, G's Aisors. After Timur's wholesale slaughter around 1400 the survivors fled to Kurdistan. There were massacres by Kurds in 1843 and 1845 and great distress from the 1914 – 18 war. To avoid quarrels they had made their celibate Patriarchate Hereditary – uncle to nephew – under the title Mar Shimun. Luke was in charge of a British Political Mission in Tiflis in 1920 and was able to dole out some relief to the Assyrians from the Lord Mayor's Fund for the Armenians.

No wonder one got a bit confused between the Armenian priest with his map and the Aisorian priest with his ivory. It seems the alabaster copy of the latter could be a plaster cast, but how could powdered alabaster help to copy a map?

Shimun sounds like a form of Simon (see *R.M.* p 91), a name that arouses interest as there are several Simons in the gospels. The new Chambers dictionary left by a fellow lodger has a names section: "Simon, Simeon: (Hebrew) perhaps hearing: perhaps also (Greek) snub-nosed". The latter is surprising, Socrates was described as snub-nosed; and is the Hebrew only "perhaps"? In Genesis 29.33,Leah says of her second son: "Because the Lord hath heard that I was hated, he hath therefore given me this son also: and she called his name Simeon". Marginal note: "That is, hearing".

According to the Boolmarshano the first passive force descending from the Prime Source can be called "Good". The second backward flowing or ascending active force striving to reblend with its source must be called "Evil". The third independent World force is only the result of the clash everywhere of the other two fundamental forces. But when you seem near to getting logical definitions out of Beelzebub, they are liable to slip through your fingers and you are not sure how to take them.

Makary's discovery came to be used by man for "self-calming", justifying complacency; was he therefore to blame? On Wednesday 15th May 1974, 22 Jewish schoolchildren died as hostages at Maalat, and on rereading the chapter "***Justice***" an idea came about who Makary might represent, rather indeterminate so it cannot be told here. But an odd parallel presented itself later.

Some of the world's present troubles can be laid at the door of another M.K., Maynard Keynes (1883 – 1946). Governments have learned from him all too well how to avoid mass unemployment by manipulating credit, but the longer result is accelerating inflation and continually rising expectations. People who have only known conditions of shortage of labour do not realise how lucky they are to have jobs, seen in a context of 1930 or of the city slums of developing countries.

Long continued security in Britain has led to more and more demands till we seem to have achieved the dictatorship of the proletariat, that is of the Trade Unions. Russia has the dictatorship but not of the proletariat, though it sounds like a "producer's market" – the consumer can take it or leave it.

The gospel of that M.K. reversed, Karl Marx, is not as readable as the original ones. One cannot deny that his economic reading of history has force, though surely other things are important too; but his prophecy of a millenium and the withering away of the state when power passed to the factory workers was not so trustworthy. Geography does not go away and nationalist rivalries remain. History moves on and there are the new "post-industrial" problems of shortages of materials, land and water. Too many competing countries need to industrialise to employ their exploding populations and must export to buy food and materials which are getting scarcer. City-based governments generally do run into trouble over agriculture, supplies of food for their urban majority supporters. Now oil price rises have accentuated chronic balance of payments troubles to the point of absurdity.

So was admiration for Keynes a mistake? Is he to be blamed? As with Makary, not necessarily. The mistake is complacency in resting content with any theory; one feels if Keynes were living now he would see the new problems and be looking for further answers, not necessarily economic, more moral and psychological.

The Pensions Paradox. In relatively stable conditions the individual can save for his old age, but on a national scale it is not easy "to put money into the future". The funds of private pension schemes and insurance companies pile up and cannot find enough secure and profitable investment, hence the scramble into the ugly and unpopular property developments. The state evidently recognises that pensioners are really maintained by the current working population for each increase of pensions is accompanied by a less publicised increase in insurance stamps.

The Burden of Dependency. One felt that the working population was having to maintain an increasing proportion of dependents. However, Family Planning magazine for 2.7.74 says that for England and Wales the decade of highest total births was 1901–1910, so the proportion of the population over 65 has now about reached its peak and should level off. An article in the January 1975 issue says the proportion of children has fallen steadily so the combined burden of old and young is not changing so very much. This does not seem to allow for people retiring earlier and children staying longer at school with more going on to higher education. One feels a good deal of the extra educational years are paid for by more mothers going to work outside the home. The increase in part-time jobs shows the need.

The population "of working age" can carry the burden more easily if their work is made more effective by good management and by maintaining and improving the capital stock, but it is not so easy in an overcrowded country to find new investment which does not have serious disadvantages (witness the protests against new airports or motorway routes). Maintaining the stock of houses is good provision for the future but we do not seem very successful at it. Investment abroad has served us well in the past in paying for imports; threats of local nationalisation add to present risks. Now the Arabs are buying **us** up with their huge oil revenues which also do not know what to do with themselves. If only they would set up a Carnegie Trust, a Rockefeller or a Ford Foundation! The character, health and knowledge or our population is also a form of capital, but do we go about caring for them in the right way?

After unloading of those grumbles, with apologies, here are a few small points. It could be that G invented his enneagram diagram in a spell of inspiration "some rainy afternoon". For someone familiar with Islamic geometric pattens (the star is an emblem of the Deity, reports Walter Crane), after drawing a nine point star of three interlacing triangles, it is only necessary to shift two lines to get the figure for the recurring one seventh decimal. The properties of numbers are wonderful.

In the chapter "***Religion***" the group of seven beings (p 721) in Tibet was taken to point to the seven deacons appointed in Acts 6, of whom Stephen, the first martyr, was the chief. The Almznoshinoo was "Virgin's son she knew". There is controversy over whether the Almah in Isaiah 7.14 "a virgin shall conceive" should be translated "virgin" or just "young woman". In "***Purgatory***" (p 803) London-Phu-Phu-Klé was taken as Joseph Joseph clue.

5. *Suez – and Sinai*

Diary has a blank but memory insists it was during the Suez crisis of 1956 and the hounding of Eden that this old letter from my father turned up, giving a feeling of interconnectedness of great and small events.

"H.M.S. Centurion. At sea off Cape Garda Fui (Somalia). 29th March, 1894.

.....our captain has made himself very pleasant to the Canal officials and several of them came on board and went down the canal with us. The result of this was that all steamers in the canal were made to haul into the bank to let us pass so we went along very comfortably....(various details). The canal is a fine study of perspective being very straight''. He seems to have enjoyed cricket in every port, e.g. against the Telegraph clerks at Suez. At another ''we won our cricket match easily but I did not contribute to this result as I a made a big round O and did not bowl.... some diving boys came off and one undertook to go under the ship, but I do not think he did it, still they picked up pennies etc. very well''. In the Centurion, a small battleship, flagship of the China squadron, they watched the war between Japan and China and the capture of Wei-hai-wei.

Diary does record that the Egyptian nationalisation of the Suez canal in 1956 was less than six weeks after the ceremonies celebrating the end of the British Occupation of the Canal Zone, something one had forgotten. Should we be suffering from the oil-producing countries' monopolistic raising of prices, if our forces had not been withdrawn from the Persian Gulf to economize? Perhaps all the ''hauling down the flag'' has been necessary, but one wishes Britain could still at least be a good moral example, and ''export education''. Alas the wreckers are at work at home too. It is easier to destroy than to build.

Our father was also on the China station as second in command of the Vengance during part of the Russo-Japanese war of 1904-5. The Readers' Digest of September 1972 told the sad story of the Russian naval misfortunes and inefficiencies in that war. Their best admiral Makarov was lost when his flagship was blown up by a mine. A second Pacific squadron with inexperienced crews was sent round the world from the Baltic. There was a disastrous battle against the redoubtable Japanese Admiral Togo. The Russian admiral was unconscious from wounds; to save useless further loss of life the commanders surrendered.

As scapegoats for their own deficiencies the bureaucrats at home called for the court-martialling of the commanders. The Czar commuted their death sentences but they served a long term in prison. Because of the name one wonders if Gurdjieff had this in mind when he wrote his stories satirising subjective morality, one being about Lt. Makarov who shot himself because he could not pay his gambling debt to a card sharper (*R.M.* p 75).

May we return to Sir Anthony Eden? Life seems to have introduced a good man Anthonies, the latest an Anthony Cooper (co-operate?). So one wondered if there was anything specially interesting about St. Anthony with his lion and his temptations, a favourite subject for painters. "Father of Christian Monachism", his dates are given as circa 250 – 350 A.D. Centenarians are unusual among historical characters. The chief source is his life by St. Athanasius, c. 298 – 373 A.D., bishop of Alexandria, who came under Anthony's influence "at some period" – rather vague.

The other "founder of Christian cenobitical life" (in communities as apposed to hermits) is St. Pachomius, probably 292 – 346 A.D., who organised a number of monasteries for men and one for women, also in Egypt.

Legends can be cryptograms to be decoded, so one begins to phantasy that the names Mark and Anthony run together, particularly in an Egyptian context. There is a tradition that St. Mark was the first bishop of Alexandria, and one would like to think of an Anthony in the first century as a link between the earlier ascetics – the Therapeutae – and the first Christian hermits or desert dwellers (eremia – desert).

Plutarch's life of Mark Antony is said to be one of the best of his "Parallel Lives" (three volumes in Penguin Classics). The picture of Cleopatra at the window of her refuge hauling the dying Antony up with ropes is indeed dramatic.

Who was Katherine of Alexandria, removed from the calendar of saints by the Pope in 1959 because her legends are dubious? They include a mystical betrothal, a disputation before the emperor Maximin in about 313 A.D., and the connection with the wheel. She was to be tortured on an engine of four spiked wheels but the cords broke and the machine fell apart.

It seems someone took the trouble to bury her on the mountain called Jebel Katherin in the Sinai peninsula, but in the 10th century the desolate little chapel was no longer felt to be safe and her remains were brought down to the monastery built and embellished by orders of Justinian in honour of the Virgin, but renamed after Katherine.

The name Catherine with its many variants comes from the

Greek Aikaterine, of unknown origin; it was later assimilated to katharos, pure, says Chambers dictionary. This is the word in "Blessed are the pure in heart: for they shall see God".

In the early centuries A.D. the Sinai peninsula was more habitable than it is now, and there was a bishopric at Pharan, with churches and convents and many anchorites living in caves. The Moslems left Justinian's monastery in peace and were allowed to build a mosque within its high walls; being in their territory its mosaics and art treasures escaped the Christian destruction of images under the Byzantine emperor Leo the Isaurian, who ruled 717 – 740 A.D.

Body snatching did occur, for the Venetians claim to have carried off the remains of St. Mark from Alexandria in the 9th century, and the inhabitants of Bari stole St. Nicolas (Santa Claus) from Myra in Asia Minor in 1087.

One would like to push Katherine back to the 1st century A.D. and connect her also in some way with the community of Therapeutae on Lake Mareotis near Alexandria, described by Philo Judaeus in "On the Contemplative Life". The Greek for contemplation is theoria, from thea, spectacle, the same origin as theatre. Therapeuo – heal, also serve, wait on, so servants of God and healers of the soul rather than the body. Eusebius, the church historian, kept interest in this community alive by claiming them as early converts of St. Mark's.

Their diet as described is so austere that one wonders if it could support health; one suspects literary exaggeration. Philo takes the opportunity of contrasting some very licentious feasts as well as belittling the Symposia of Plato and Xenophon. The treatise also has the first known use of the word monasterion, a consecrated room in each house "called a sanctuary or closet and closeted in this they are initiated into the mysteries of the sacred life". (Philo, Volume IX in the Loeb Classical Library, translated by F. H. Colson, late fellow of St. John's College, Cambridge: first printed 1941). "But thou, when thou prayest, enter into thy closet, and when thou hast shut thy door, pray to thy Father which is in secret – and thy Father which seeth in secret shall reward thee openly" Matthew 6.6.

Philo, whose birth is put variously from 30 to 10 B.C., his date of death being unknown, belonged to one of the leading Jewish families of Alexandria. His father, or brother, Alexander was Alabarch, believed to mean tax farmer of the Arab side of the Nile; a nephew Tiberius Alexander became thoroughly Romanized and served as Procurator of Judaea about A.D. 46, and as Governor of Alexandria under Nero. When the legions in Palestine declared Vespasian emperor, Tiberius brought Egypt over to Vespasian; he was second in command to Titus at the siege of Jerusalem in A.D. 70.

Philo is the culmination of the Judaeo-Alexandrine school of philosophy; he interpreted the Jewish scriptures as psychological allegories. The article on Jewish philosophy says he had no Jewish successors, but the Fathers of the Church almost adopted him as their own.

Subsidence has sunk parts of ancient Alexandria under the sea, including the site of the Pharos, the world's first lighthouse, and the Lochias promontory on which the royal palaces stood. Alexander laid out his city in 332 B.C. near an Egyptian townlet of fishers and pirates, called Rhacotis. He never returned to it alive, though his mausoleum was there. He was probably 32 when he died. Alexandria flourished under the Ptolemies and became a centre of learning. The texts of Homer were edited there and the Septuagint, the Greek version of the Old Testament, was, according to Josephus, translated there on the island.

As mentioned a number of times by Josephus (e.g. Antiquities XIII.3.1.) the Egyptian Jews had their own temple at Leontopolis in the country Bubastis, near the modern Zagazig. He says it was copied from the Jerusalem temple but smaller, and was built on an artificial mound with a steep drop from the battlements at the back. Flinders Petrie describes its excavation in "Egypt and Israel", published in 1911 by the Society for Promoting Christian Knowledge. After the fall of Jerusalem the Sicarii, (who were perhaps a bit like the I.R.A.) tried to raise a revolt in Egypt; as a result this temple was despoiled and shut up "so that there remained no longer the least footsteps of any divine worship that had been in that place".

Bubastis was a lion-headed goddess to whom cats were also sacred. It is intriguing to ponder why lions should be connected with St. Mark. They seem to be met everywhere and not only under Nero. The legends of the Desert Fathers have many friendly lions, as do fairy tales. Two famous lions; Leonardo da Vinci, Leo Tolstoy.

Ignatius, bishop of Antioch in Syria, shows such extraordinary enthusiasm for martyrdom by the wild beasts in the amphitheatre that one wonders if the lions were used as a type for intentional suffering in general. He wrote to the Roman Church, "Suffer me to be eaten by the beasts, through whom I can attain to God.... Rather entice the wild beasts that they may become my tomb and leave no trace of my body, that when I fall asleep I be not burdensome to any. Then shall I be truly a disciple of Jesus Christ, when the world shall not even see my body".

Another first use, the word "leopard". He was travelling "bound to ten 'leopards' (that is, a company of soldiers).... I long for the beasts that are prepared for me...the kingdoms of this world shall profit me nothing....the pains of birth are upon me". He is thought to have been martyred under Trajan (ruled 98 – 117 A.D.). The quotations are taken from the translation by Kirsopp Lake, 1912, in Volume I of the Apostolic Fathers, Loeb Classical Library, pp 231–3.

6. Myers

Someone named Myers mistook his Channel crossing and hastened back to Paris hoping for one more day at Mr. Gurdjieff's flat. It seems he was refused and Mr. G said: "he very naıve, he think he can come back without work". This came to mean something different: F. W.H. Myers (1843–1901) and the English Psychical Researchers who promised to try to "come back", that is, communicate after their death. So one of the aims of Gurdjieff's strenuous life was seen as being to leave behind him prepared people and a trail of detective clues, thoughts "discernible only with the lapse of time" (*R.M.* p 7), whose unravelling with the help of the "unconscious" – recognising his clipped and painted sparrows – would be part of a kind of a demonstration of Resurrection or whatever you call the afterlife. "It can never be proved, but you can become convinced".

In fairness to the English workers it should be said Dr. Kenneth Walker in "*The Unconscious Mind*" reports that literary cross-correspondences between the scripts of different automatic writers are held to come from Myers; one has seen advertised a book called "*The Return of Arthur*" (Conan Doyle, 1859–1930); and Podmore was the maiden name of the mother of two little boys living down the road. Frank Podmore 1856–1910, psychologist associated with Myers and Edmund Gurney in writing "*Phantasms of the Living*" 1886, was found drowned near Malvern. Gurney, 1847–1888, died of an overdose of narcotic medicine.

Psychical research, spiritualism, theosophy, the psychology of the unconscious, Gurdjieff, may all be part of a general movement of ideas, or plan, in the same direction. Geology and evolution, archaeology, study of oriental scriptures and comparative religion have each widened our perspective. What is our generation's contribution, or the next step? To bring the threads together in a synthesis on the human situation?

It may as well be confessed that this present writing, though admittedly limited and coloured by the head through which it passes, is felt to belong to a "continuation" of Gurdjieff's Third Series of writings which he did not complete in his lifetime. "Interpretations of G's riddles" have been scattered all through, but here are some possible "literary cross-correspondences". Readers may well find others, for there are probably more.

Huckleberry Finn (first published 1885), p 213 Puffin Books: "I'd noticed that Providence always did put the right words in my mouth, if I left it alone. When I got half-way, first one hound and then another got up and went for me, and of course I stopped and faced them, and kept still" – till fifteen surrounded him, a-barking and howling. A nigger woman came tearing out of the kitchen with a rolling pin and stopped them, and half came back wagging their tails to make friends.

Read G's story of the Kurd sheepdogs in *Remarkable Men*, p 94.

It is so lively and circumstantial it must have really happened? Well, maybe it did, but notice "in all about fifteen sheepdogs".

Mark Twain's chapter starts off "When I got there it was all still and Sunday-like .... and there was them kind of faint dronings of bugs....that makes it seem so lonesome and like everybody's dead and gone; and if a breeze fans along and quivers the leaves, it makes you feel mournful, because you feel like it's spirits whispering – spirits that's been dead ever so many years – and you always think they're talking about *you*".

Huckleberry Finn illustrates the contrast which G makes in the chapter ***Bogachevsky*** between subjective and objective morality, for example when Huck thought he ought to give up sin and hand over the run-away nigger, but found he couldn't (p 208). "All right, then, I'll go to hell"; he tore up the letter, and set out to steal Jim out of slavery again, "because as long as I was in, and in for good, I might as well go the whole hog". It is tempting also to put in how when he was hiding and dasn't scratch, he got to itching in eleven different places (p 15). The parallel with G's "if you go on a spree then go the whole hog including the postage (***All and Everything*** p 37) may of course be quite accidental, but there is "a strong almost unbearable itch" on the same page. Earlier associations to this phrase were "the Holy Ghost Age" and that Berlin is on the river Spree.

Gorbakoun, who in the chapter ***Bogachevsky*** accidentally shot G in the leg, was for a long time thought to represent Roger Bacon as inventor of gunpowder; later he was felt to indicate Bakunin (1814–1876), and the spate of terrorist political assassinations around 1900.

The Journals of Kierkegaard (1813–1855):
"Just as the top layer in a case of herrings is crushed and spoilt, and the fruit next the crate....so too in every generation there are certain men who are on the outside, and are made to suffer from the packing case, who only protect those who are in the middle....when in a generation storms begin to gather, individuals of my type appear". Is it relevant to G's story of the rotting barrels of herrings in ***"The Material Question"*** (**R.M.** p 267)?

Though G was so rude about European literature one would

think he must have been interested in Tolstoy, and Dostoievsky (1821–1881). In "***The Brothers Karamazov***" there is an incident of a boy lying down on a railway track to let a train thunder over him, for a dare, and another about a toy copper cannon. One feels it might have suggested G's vivid story about lying on the firing range for "a duel with cannon", in Piotr Karpenko, with its experience of fear. Like the ez-ezounavouran in this chapter, Dostoievsky's saint Zossima had been in the army.

* * * * * * *

Xenophon: Memorabilia of Socrates Book I. Ch. III, against the dangers of being enslaved by beautiful people: "Do you not know that the animal, which they call a handsome and beautiful object, is so much more formidable than the Tarantula (phalangia), as those insects instil something when they touch the body, but this creature, without even touching, but if a person only looks at it, though from a very great distance, instils something of such potency, as to drive people mad...I advise you, Xenophon, whenever you see any handsome person, to flee without looking behind you." A footnote doubts whether the tarantula bite really has the effects attributed to it. The translation is by the Rev. J.S. Watson, Bohn, 1862. The phalanga bite in ***Remarkable Men*** is on page 96 in the chapter "***Mr. X or Captain Pogossian***".

One cannot resist quoting the dictionary: "Tarantism, dancing mania, specially in S. Italy, among people who (thought they) had been bitten by the Tarantula (from the Italian town of Taranto, Latin Tarentum)". Elsewhere it appears that Tarentum was Taras, the later Pythagorean headquarters. Could the Pythagoreans be one of Gurdjieff's many brotherhoods? Did they dance? The dancing mania gives a queer feeling that influences from the remote past might have been acting through "the collective unconscious".

A rather earlier Etruscan tomb painting of the 6th century B.C. shows a dancer with his head going one way and feet the other, and arm uncomfortably bent at right angles; one wonders if G could have borrowed an idea for his movements from this source. It is illustrated in D.H. Lawrence ***"Mornings in Mexico"*** and

"Etruscan Places" (Penguin). The best of these Etruscan paintings date from about the time when Pythagoras was teaching in the south. Is it too much to draw from this, and G's chapter on *"Art"*, which mentions Pythagoras, that, apart from Laws of Sevenfoldness and cunning "otherwises", there may be a duty for people privileged to seek "higher development", to contribute quality, salt, to ordinary life in fields like entertainment, song and dance, architecture, painting and literature, education, medicine, engineering and crafts – any field for which they have some gift and for which they can acquire training; or just in standards of conduct and daily intercourse? Dance and art can be worship.

Pythagoras (one of the few historical names in Beelzebub) and his followers are one of the subjects which have exercised a peculiar fascination; other such are Harran (because of Laban, and Laban notation for movements), the Therapeutae, the Druids, Mithraism. One never seems to assimilate properly what information one does meet about them. Apparently the elder Pliny saw similarity between the teachings of the Magi and the Druids (Mead, Vol. III, p 194); as hereditary learned castes both must be like the ancient Brahmins. One wonders if some of Pythagoras' teaching got into the oral traditions of the Druids with their long years of education. At least as regards the question whether Pythagoras influenced Etruscan art – another painting shows a piper playing two pipes – we do know he studied the musical scale and is reputed to have originated the word "harmony" from a root "to join". He also invented the word "philosophy".

Here is a touch about the Pythagoreans which does appeal. It is from Cicero (106 – 43 B.C.) "On Old Age" translated by Michael Grant for Penguin Classics. Cicero was 62 when he wrote it, but the essay is put into the mouth of Cato the Elder at 84, in 150 B.C. "Age has to fought against....the mind and spirit need even more attention than the body, for old age easily extinguishes them ..... just as I like a young man to have something old about him, so I approve of the old man who has a touch of youth.... I am an active student of Greek literature; and to keep my memory in training I adopt the practice of the Pythagoreans and, every evening, run over in my mind all that I have said and heard and done during the day". So the "daily retrospect" has a long history. Further on Cato says "Pythagoras forbids us to desert life's sentry post till God, our commander, has given the word".

No evidence has been found to show that the Pythagoreans danced, but the Therapeutae, who may be Neo-pythagoreans, are thought to have done so at their occasional festal meeting and vigil. After an address and hymn-singing and the frugal meal of bread, salt and hyssop with water to drink, the men and women form separate choirs and sing more hymns, hands and feet keeping time and "rapt with enthusiasm reproduce sometimes the lyrics of the procession, sometimes of the halt and of the wheeling and counter-wheeling of a choric dance". At sunrise they face the east, "stretch their hands up to heaven and pray for bright days and knowledge of the truth and the power of keen sighted thinking" (Philo, Contemplative Life, 84, 89).
It could be a link in traditions which run through to the Mevlevi dervishes and Gurdjieff's development of sacred dances as a major element in his method. In the chapter *"Ekim Bey", R.M.* p 179, he writes of standing on the bridge between Pera and Stamboul pondered on the "significance of the continuous movement of the whirling dervishes, which at first glance seems automatic".

* * * * * * *

In connection with G's insistence that man is a machine, and on his "mechanicity", a passage from Xenophon's Memorabilia (Book IV, Ch. VII) is interesting. He says that Socrates tried to render his followers skilful – mekhanikos. The learning of physical skills and crafts is a feature of G's method.

Two minor possible correspondences are: ***Pinocchio,*** first published 1883: "In this world we should accustom ourselves from childhood to like and to eat everything, for there is no saying what may happen to us". "Do not throw it away: in this world everything may be of use". ***Petonius*** "to describe someone in a rage says 'with her thumb bitten to danger point'."

Perhaps this is going too far, a mere fragment preserved by being quoted in some other author (p 167 in Penguin Petronius); still he is significant for his Rabelaisian humour.

The first reference is to the Persian dervish, advising against artificial mastication and artificial breathing; ''At your age it is better not to chew at all, but to swallow whole pieces, even bones if possible, to give work to your stomach''(*R.M.* p 186). It follows the terrifying saying: ''Let God kill him who himself does not know and yet presumes to show others the way to the doors of His Kingdom''.

The morning after recopying the Etruscan paragraphs, and adding the dance of the Therapeutae, there was a present. It was in checking on how Vitvitskaia ''either from rage or exhaustion or for some other reason'' bit her finger so hard she nearly severed it from her hand, while she was puzzling over the power of the monotonous music they heard at a monastery in Turkestan, not accessible to everyone (*R.M.* pp 128–133). Gurdjieff told her he ''had been among the Essenes, most of whom are Jews, and that by means of very ancient Hebraic music and songs they had made plants grow in half an hour''.

Whatever it all means, that is some confirmation for connecting Gurdjieff's music and movements with the Therapeutae who are classed with the Essenes. The previous week had been somewhat dominated by a young man who rang at the door applying for a room. He gave his name as George Calliste which rather obviously translates into George's callisthenics. On the last page of Philo's Contemplative Life, after the sunrise prayer the Therapeutae ''depart each to his private sanctuary'' to ''till the field of their wonted philosophy''. The word on the Greek page opposite caught the eye ''george....''. Why, one never thought of looking up the name George! Perhaps it does mean something like ploughman. The dictionary gave ''husbandman'', so that was added to the spelling section.

''Zeroes in cheque book'' were often in mind. They came to mean the double o's of made-up names in Beelzebub, such as Pooloodjistius, the tutor to Beelzebub's two sons (p 1121 Justice). His name recalls Pelagius, British theologian who got involved in arguments with the first St. Augustine (of Hippo in N. Africa; born in 354 A.D., he died in 430 during the Vandal siege) over free-will, pre-destination and grace. The opinions of Pelagius were condemned. He denied original sin and said we are free to choose and so are responsible. Later, semipelagianism said the human will ***co-operated*** with the divine will, which seems a good solution.

Much later the zeroes came to mean statistics in Josephus' two books which are a sort of "check-book" for the history of New Testament times. Petrie's S.P.C.K. book, which looked so old-fashioned it was once nearly thrown away, proved exceptionally useful. It gave the first information about the Egyptian Jewish temple which might have been the scene of the death of a "zig-zag idiot" by a fall from the battlements in a high wind while observing an eclipse of the moon. There is some echo also of the temptation of Jesus on a pinnacle of the temple. There seemed no way to find out more except from Petrie's source, Josephus. When the fact that the Greek title of his "Jewish Antiquities" was Ioudaike Archaiologia finally registered, it seemed Josephus could be Gurdjieff's Archaeologist Professor Skridlov, and a copy must be procured, complicated by the postal strike of 1971.

Editions of Josephus come in very small print, not encouraging. This one was translated by William Whiston, Professor of Mathematics in the University of Cambridge, and immediate successor of Isaac Newton. His footnotes are interesting. One says of an eclipse shortly before the death of Herod the Great: "this eclipse of the moon (which is the only eclipse mentioned by Josephus) is of the greatest consequence for the determination of the time for the death of Herod and Antipater, and for the birth and entire chronology of Jesus Christ. It happened March 13th, in the year of the Julian period 4710, and the 4th year before the Christian era". (Antiquities XVII.6.4). Perhaps he or Newton made the calculation? Tertullian says in the Apology (21.20), that the darkness at the crucifixion was attributed by the Jews to an eclipse.

A footnote about Josephus' shipwreck says: "It has been

thought that the number of Paul and his companions on ship board, (Acts 27.37) which are 276 in our copies, are too many; wheras we find here that Josephus and his companions, a very few years after the other, were about 600". (Life, 3).

Josephus' statistics may qualify as intentional inexactitudes. He adds 100 years to each of the ages in Genesis at which the generations from Noah to Abraham beget their sons, and does remarkable things to the dimensions of Solomon's temple. In two places he describes a tumult at the Passover in which many were trampled as the crowd tried to get out of the temple; in his earlier work "The Jewish War" II.XII.I, he gives the number as 10,000: in Antiquities XX.V.3 the number becomes 20,000. Eusebius repeats this story in his much-quoted "Ecclesiastical History" (II,XIX.), but gives the number as 30,000. In our Glasgow Ibrox Park football crowd disaster on staircase 13 the number fatally crushed was 66.

Eusebius does not repeat Josephus' next paragraph in which some of those who raised the Passover tumult then "robbed Stephanus, a servant of Caesar, as he was journeying, and plundered him of all that he had with him", setting off more trouble. A possible date for this is Pharmuthi 19 – April 14th A.D. 51, when Cumanus was procurator. A similar name is met in Philo's Flaccus, where the governor is arrested at a feast given by "Stephanio, one of the freedmen of Tiberius Caesar". The arrest was ordered by Gaius (Caligula), emperor from 37 to 41 A.D.

Eusebius was bishop of the Caesarea which is a seaport of Samaria; he was leader of the moderates at the Council of Nicaea, and clearly an able man. The churches' history has not been distinguished by love for their enemies and Eusebius duly attacks the heretics, starting with the Samaritan Simon Magus (Acts Ch. 8), father of Gnosticism.

The stories about Simon are very confusing. He is said to have been called Faustus, fortunate, when in Rome, and so to be the original of the medieval Faust legend. He learned magic in Egypt. He called himself the Standing One, an incarnation of God the Father, and was accompanied by a Helena rescued from a brothel in Tyre, who represented the fallen Thought of God. Eusebius (II.14) says Simon "undertook a great journey across the sea, and went off in flight from east to west". He had success in Rome until the great and mighty Peter "brought the costly merchandise of the spiritual light from the east to the dwellers in the west", and Simon's power was extinguished together with the fellow himself (Loeb translation by Kirsopp Lake). There are conflicting legends about the manner of his death.

One wonders if the title Magus implies any connection with the Persian traditions or Mithraism. Somehow one got the idea that Simon might really have been a "good" Samaritan and played a role similar in some way to Gurdjieff's; and that he may have perished in a ship wreck on a voyage to or from Rome, possibly around the time of Caligula's assassination. The succour he gave to the man who fell among thieves would have been "on the other side", welcoming him the the "inn" after death, or preparing a place in the Father's mansions.

* * * * * * *

It was surprising to find a British warship in Mme de Hartmann's account (Thomas de Hartmann "*Our Life with Mr. Gurdjieff*", p 83) of her perilous trip to Essentuki in 1919 that was reminiscent of the British warship in G's chapter ***Pogossian***. Does it mean he felt his senior pupils were fellow seekers? Are not his "Seekers of the Truth" really an invisibly-linked brotherhood of seekers everywhere and throughout history? There is an idea that amid the dangers, destructions and chaos of war or revolution remarkable "coincidences" happen more easily, a principle illustrated by Pasternak in his "Dr. Zhivago".

The chapter ***Ekim Bey*** suggests Ouspensky who helped Gurdjieff earn money in Constantinople when they were refugees in 1920. Born in 1878 (died 1947), Ouspensky was only a year or so younger and evidently already knew a great deal when he met G. G's story of diving for coins and retrieving a rosary from the sea bottom found a possible explanation in the psychoanalysts' use of "diving into the sea" as an analogy for diving into the (collective) unconscious.

The extraordinary sensitivity to tiny movements of the hand, given as an explanation of magicians' tricks in the same chapter (**R.M.** p 193) found an echo in quite a different context, the life of Helen Keller (1880 – 1968) who was blind and deaf from the age of 19 months. While she was holding the hand of her devoted teacher Anne Sullivan she would turn her head to a speaker and smile as if she heard; to a less extent she could do it holding someone else's hand but without a hand she gave no response. In the story of her life (1903) she says that one of her Swiss ancestors was the first teacher of the deaf at Zurich, and wrote a book about it – "rather a singular coincidence". To someone with theories about the possible influence of ancestors, this is striking.

Ekim Bey is described as telling fortunes by holding the client's hand as he moved it over the letters of the alphabet; for example: "The first letter of your name is . . .". Having obtained the letters S, T, and E, he could guess that the name was Stephen.

Colin Wilson in "The Occult" retells some of the colourful early life of Mme Helena Petrovna Blavatsky (1831 – 1891), founder of the Theosophical Society and a puzzling mixer of conjuring tricks with genuine powers. She had been a circus bare-back rider and had managed an artificial flower factory in Tiflis. In ***Remarkable Men*** (p 141) G says he earned money in New Bukhara by making artificial paper flowers; at this time he met Soloviev by intervening in a fight, rather like the incident of the fight in Pogossian; on page 144 we hear how Soloviev lost his head over a bare-back circus rider. This is not inconsistent with the idea that Soloviev may represent Rudolf Steiner as he was a theosophist before breaking away to found his own anthroposophical movement. (see above, p 24).

Closer study of "***Meetings with Remarkable Men***", shows a definite tendency to repetitions which looks deliberate. Making artificial flowers also has two mentions, the first on p136 at New Samarkand. There are also two references (pp 73 and

121) to a dervish of Broussa, south of Constantinople. The first comes after an account of how G's teacher Bogachevsky joined the Essene brotherhood, and says G learned much about his extraordinary life during this period from the tales of this Turkish dervish in Broussa. He might be Dio of Prusa (the old name), called Chrysostom – golden mouthed, who lived from about 40 to 120 A.D. Dio left some eighty Discourses, of which the Euboean is praised. It describes how he was shipwrecked on his wanderings and was succoured by a countryman leading an idyllic life; Dio was able to share in a wedding feast for which the fatted pig was just ready. Then he discusses suitable employment for the poor in cities and attacks permissiveness and the legalisation of brothels.

7. *Josephine Butler, and Glastonbury*

A current event, which may have given Gurdjieff material for his chapter "*America*" and for the story of Vitvitskaia in ***Remarkable Men***, was the report in 1927 of the Experts' Committee of the League of Nations on the Traffic in Women and Children – the White Slave Trade. This was the culmination of the crusade by Mrs. Josephine Butler (née Grey, 1828 – 1906) against the injustices of the system, instituted by Napoleon, of licensed brothels and compulsory medical inspection of prostitutes (not the men), which did not in fact reduce the incidence of veneral disease. She recommended free voluntary clinics as a better answer.

From 1866 – 1882 her husband George Butler was principal of Liverpool college. "Among its eight to nine hundred pupils there were Greeks, Armenians, Jews . . . .". Could this be the "technical institute of marine engineering at Liverpool", in ***Remarkable Men***, p 106? In a dream of Jung's, Liverpool stood for the pool of life; it can also be "spelt" pull of the book – livre. The Butlers had three sons but their one little daughter Evangeline died from a fall from an upper landing when Mr. Butler was Vice-Principal of Cheltenham College.

A text about another nineteenth century woman pioneer comes in a letter to the Daily Telegraph (17.5.74) from Wargrave:

"Florence Nightingale was a tiger". "She was born years ahead of her time, but she was one of those people whom God, or fate, or call it what you will, put a finger upon and said 'This you will do'". (She was born in Florence and named after that city).

That there was a mystical element in Mrs. Butler's religion is suggested both by her charge that no one should write of her own personal or spiritual life and experiences, and by the influence she had on the men of her time. Frederick Myers (father of F.W.H. Myers) wrote that she "introduced him to Christianity by an inner door, not to its encumbering forms and dogmas but to its heart of fire". Dame Katherine Furse (founder of the V.A.D. Voluntary Aid Detachment – in September, 1914, Director of the Women's Royal Naval Service 1917 – 1919, and subsequently a worker for the Boy Scout and Girl Guide movements) found among the papers of her father John Addington Symonds one on "Women who have most influenced me". The list was headed by the name of Josephine Butler.

The information is taken from a book written, with an assistant, for the centenary of Mrs. Butler's birth by Millicent Garrett Fawcett, the women's suffrage leader. Dame Millicent (1847 – 1929) was a younger sister of Dr. Elizabeth Garrett Anderson, the first English woman doctor. (The first American, Dr. Mary Putnam Jacobi, qualified slightly earlier). She was the widow of Henry Fawcett (1832 – 1884) the Postmaster General who introduced parcel post, 6d (old penny) telegrams, postal orders, and other improvements. He was blinded at 25 by his own father in a shooting accident, but determined to show it would not prevent him following his chosen career. The Fawcetts first met at a party where everyone was discussing the news of Abraham Lincoln's assassination. Milly said the misfortune was greater than the loss of any of the crowned heads of Europe, and Henry at once asked to be introduced to her.

What became of their daughter Philippa who as a Newnham student was placed "above the Senior Wrangler" (first in the Cambridge Mathematical Tripos) in 1890? During the Boer War 105,000 refugee Boer women and children were gathered in 34 Concentration Camps hastily set up in 1900 and 1901; conditions were very bad, epidemics raged both within and without the camps; the pro-Boer sympathisers in England made a great fuss and feelings ran very high. It seems a prophetic foretaste of twentieth century problems. (The biography of Mrs. Fawcett by Ray Strachey was written in 1929–30).

The Government asked Mrs. Fawcett to head a commission of six ladies, including two doctors and a nurse, to investigate and recommend immediate practical measures. In ten days she was ready and sailed in a troopship, taking Philippa as her "maid". The Commissioners lived for four months in a railway carriage, and were able to make considerable improvements. One thing they could praise in the camps was the improvised schooling which was welcomed by the refugees. After the end of the war in 1902 Philippa went back to S. Africa to help in organizing elementary education; in 1905 she became assistant to the Director of Education for London County Council, living with her mother and aunt, and sharing in the continuing suffrage struggle. In January 1918 the Representation of the People Bill passed the Lords, giving votes to women householders, and the wives of men householders, who were over 30. "Votes for Flappers", i.e. at 21 as for men, came in 1928.

Dame Millicent and her sister Miss Agnes Garrett visited our school which was in former Garrett houses at Aldeburgh, Suffolk, in the 1920's – two tiny old ladies in bonnets. The father of the ten brothers and sisters, Newson Garrett, had owned the Snape maltings, now converted to a concert hall for the Aldeburgh festivals.

Having some lingering feminist resentments one soon noticed that there are hardly any women's names in Gurdjieff's writings – Vitvitskaia, Sheherazade, the nun Ephrosinia (***All and Everything*** p 573), the schoolgirls Sonia (p 1033), Mary and Elizabeth (p 1037). Women have played their full share in his work, so what was his reason? Herman Hesse managed to write his Magister Ludi, Glasperlenspiel, with scarcely a woman in it (till the delicious former incarnations at the end) but the pure intellectualism does make it rather heavy going.

Alexander Sutherland Neill (1883 – 1973) had his ultra-proggressive school Summerhill in a house built by another Garrett family, founders of the engineering works at Leiston. Curious is that Neill's school originally started in 1921 at Hellerau near Dresden. Gurdjieff says in his chapter "*The Material Question*" that *he* was negotiating to acquire a house at Hellerau near Dresden, that had been specially designed for the Dalcroze system, during his stay in Berlin 1920–21 with his refugee party, when the prospect arose of starting his Institute in England. However after some visits to England he finally chose France. Report has it that the British Foreign Office would not grant a visa, because he was believed to be Lama Dordjieff, who had advised the Dalai Lama against Britain.

Neill's early theories are one-sided, but he does write from long practical experience of children. He used to think delinquents were frustrated bright children, but he was sadly wrong, they are usually inferiors in intelligence and emotion. A child is primarily an egoist, he strives to compel admiration and attention. "If I can't get love, I can get hate". Criminality is revenge, it is a question of injured ego, "To pretend that I love a new pupil would be fatuous; yet the child feels that I love him because I respect his ego". Be on the children's side. Treatment is most hopeful only for the very young. (*Summerhill,* Penguin Books, pp 240–251).

What is the point of all this? Just padding, or to suggest the value of history as food for concrete thinking, or to show how lives are linked unexpectedly? The name of Virginia Woolf may be invoked for the "flow of association" style. V.D., having no children of her own family to leave things to, presented this great-niece of her life-long friend Ella, née Sieveking (whose grand-parents came to London from Hamburg) with a filigree brooch labelled "Belonged to Virginia Woolf's mother" (Mrs. Leslie Stephen), (V.D. is Violet Dickinson).

This writer's father sold the Leiston house to A. S. Neill in 1927, having unsuccessfully tried to run a "home school" there himself. In the checking of this section on 13th May, 1975 the impulse arose to write to Mrs. A. S. Neill to ask about the Hellerau house, reinforced by the appearance of her husband's name in that morning's Daily Mail, delivered exceptionally because of a strike at the Telegraph. The letter mentioned "superstitions about the connection because of another Neil, whose Scottish grandfather, originally McNeill, emigrated to Australia, and who played a part in our community at Coombe Springs."

Mrs. Neill's kind reply arrived appropriately on 30th May, father's birthday; she refers to the International School (from which Summerhill was an offshoot) and says "I have often heard Neill say that it was the place specially built for the Dalcroze dance school".

Glastonbury: There is something tantalising about the Glastonbury legend of the visit of Joseph of Arimathea, about the Druids, and Caractacus, as if Northern Europe could really have had some very early links with Christianity. What one does find is a connection between the family of Vespasian – the Flavians – and the early church in Rome, such as that one of the first catacombs was under their land.

Vespasian had been a commander in Claudius' conquest of Britain, A.D. 43 and 44. According to one account he took the Isle of Wight and penetrated to the borders of Somerset, so it is even possible that it was Vespasian's troops who destroyed the lake village near Glastonbury. Vespasian was the patron of that other Joseph, the Jewish historian Josephus, who took the name Flavius and settled in Rome in an apartment in Vespasian's own old house, where the latter had lived before he was emperor.

One of the first things which helped to register the name Vespasian was a news item, that the public urinals, which had at last been removed from the streets of Rome, were called by the citizens Vespaniani, because the soldier-emperor liked coarse jokes. Vespasian's father was a tax collector. Suetonius' "The Twelve Caesars" is full of wonders and portents: "Also a distinguished Jewish prisoner of Vespasians, Jozephus by name, insisted that he would soon be released by the very man who had now put him in fetters, and who would then be emperor".

In 69 A.D., the army in Egypt and his troops in Judaea elected Vespasian. While his troops in Italy defeated Vitellius, the third emperor to rule for a few months, since the revolt against Nero,

Vespasian went to Alexandria. "As he sat on the Tribunal, two labourers, one blind, the other lame, approached together, begging to be healed. Apparently the god Serapis had promised them in a dream that if Vespasian would consent to spit in the blind man's eyes, and touch the lame man's leg with his heel, both would be made well". Vespasian was reluctant, but his friends persuaded him and the charm worked. (Robert Graves' Penguin translation of Suetonius pp 277 and 279).

Vespasian died aged 69 in June 79 A.D., two months before the disastrous eruption which destroyed Herculaneum and Pompeii. The near-by article on Vesuvius says the explosion was preceded by some sixteen years of earthquakes of increasing severity, spreading alarm through Campania.

Cornelius Tacitus (the name does mean silent), who lived from A.D. 56 – 120, also has a connection with Britain. He wrote the life of his father-in-law Agricola, who served three times in Britain, first as a youngster under Suetonius Paulinus at the time of Boudicca's rebellion, (A.D. 60 or 61, described in Tacitus' Annals). The third time was when Vespasian sent him as Governor in A.D. 78. In seven summers of campaigning Agricola completed the conquest of North Wales and Anglesey and the North of England and penetrated far into Scotland, incurring the jealousy of Domitian by his success.

Tacitus has some zeroes too. In his Annals he says fifty thousand people were mutilated or crushed to death in the collapse of stands at a gladiatorial show in A.D. 27 during the reign of Tiberius. Tacitus says later that to suppress rumours that the burning of Rome had been instigated, "Nero fabricated scapegoats – and punished with every refinement the notoriously depraved Christians (as they were popularly called). Their originator, Christ, had been executed in Tiberius' reign by the governor of Judaea, Pontius Pilatus". Michael Grant's footnotes to his Penguin translation say "This is the only mention in pagan Latin of Pontius Pilate's action" and "Tacitus seems to hesitate (as often) between two versions. Were the Christians persecuted as incendiaries or as Christians?"

Gurdjieff's Pogossian (*R.M.* p 84) had the right eye slightly crossed. Several of the children one knew had a squint and the title of ***Quint***ilian's book is Institutio Oratoria, which echoes G's word Institute. It seemed as if his book must be procured. Vespasian created a chair of rhetoric for him. He is described as the perfect schoolmaster, kindly and sensible – dates about 35 to about 95 A.D. Among his pupils was the younger Pliny (61 or 62 to about 113 A.D., a friend of Tacitus and Suetonius) who wrote a famous letter to Trajan asking advice about the Christians, when he was governor of Bithynia. It is hard to see why Quintilian's book on the training of the orator should be relevant unless it be for passages like the discussion in Book IX.II.65 on a class of figure ''whereby we excite some suspicion to indicate that our meaning is other than our words would seem to imply''.

After the murder of Domitian in A.D. 96 by a steward named Stephanus, Rome had a long spell of good government under the adoptive emperors from Nerva till the death of Marcus Aurelius Antoninus in 180, though not without the seeds of future troubles. This period of stability is held to be largely due to the influence of the Stoic philosophy, supporting the thesis that the only hope of good government is on a foundation of personal ethics.

8. The Ark, and Ashiata

The locksmith needn't go in – too uncertain; but a suitcase which has lost its locks shows up in a dream, so perhaps it should. Pogossian becoming an assistant locksmith at the Tiflis railway station (**R.M.** pp 86–87) might suggest John Locke (1632–1704), attractive as one of the apostles of toleration. His Essay concerning Human Understanding (and its limits) was an important common-sense step in the history of philosophy. Pogossian giving up his theological training might refer to G's own experience of changing from theology to medicine.

On the other hand, Stalin's life by Isaac Don Levine (1931) says: ''In the Caucasus capitalism came with a rush''; among newly arrived, and revolutionary, workers were Michael Kalinin, later president of the Soviet Union, who found a job in the railway shops as a joiner, and Alliluiev, a locksmith, who became an ardent Bolshevik and was the father of Stalin's second wife. One of the many aliases of Stalin, whose real name was Joseph Djugashvili, was Nizheradze, which is believed also to be the title of an uncompleted chapter of Gurdjieff's Second Series.

Lenin said: "Let every kitchen maid learn to run the government" (Levine p 39). ***All and Everything*** p 1198: the coachman-cabby dressed in a cloak thrown out "by the kitchen-maid Maggie". Not much of a correspondence, but it serves to introduce the feeling that Lenin and Stalin did have knowledge of the invisible powers, they seem to give the passwords. How could the spirits help such ruthless men? The powers seem to fight on both sides, it is frightening. Are the Napoleons and Hitlers responsible, or just history puppets? Could they have chosen differently? As one cannot answer, let reference be made to G's Eternal–Hasnamuss–individuals, on p 405 in the chapter "***The Chief Culprit in the Destruction of All the Very Saintly Labours of Ashiata Shiemash***", though not simply as an appeal to authority or necessarily the last word. Tradition in the groups says the culprit Lentrohamsanin stands for Lenin, Trotsky and an Armenian communist.

Much time was spent thinking up fanciful reasons for Mr. Gurdjieff's shaven head; was it for a vow, do Buddhist monks shave their heads? Or was it just that he was going bald anyway and thought he would go the whole hog and shave the rest? One possibility is that he may have wanted to emphasise his pronounced racial type – the extreme of broadheadedness, almost flat at the back, big nose, light brown skin. It seems this shape of skull is very ancient in Armenia; the type is also rather like early Sumerean sculptures and it is possible the Sumerians migrated from Armenia into the valley of the two rivers.

This idea may have arisen from Beelzebub's remarks in the night restaurant on Montmartre (p 675) about ancient types reappearing. The "pilot", who in fact only came to the groups through ordering and reading "***All and Everything***" in Australia after Mr. G's death, was physically of the opposite extreme, tall, very thin, narrow-headed, with a slight stoop, blond – as if to show that every race has something to contribute, none has a monopoly.

G has several Persians – the young Persian in the chapter ***France***, the literary one in the introduction of the Second Series, and the Persian dervish in ***Ekim Bey.*** Candidates to have contributed to them are Zoroaster, Rumi, and Ahriman, the Devil himself, that so useful invention of "Persian dualism".

The next piece was to be about Flood stories and cuneiform tablets, but on re-reading how G's father chanted the flood song from the legend of Gilgamesh, attention was caught by the teasing work Ashokh, which G says means bard or poet (***R.M.*** p 32). It is repeated in the name of the fortune-teller Eoung-Ashokh Mardiross in "***Bogachevsky***". It is also a name in India, Ashokh Rampal, B.B.C. programmer. Could it be the same as that King Asoka; was he the one who sent Buddhist missionaries to the West? Ten minutes to fill till supper-time, where is that book on India? (H. G. Rawlinson, 1937, Cresset Press).

Yes, Asoka, emperor of Magadha from 273 – 232 B.C., (or 268 to 228 or 227). After a successful war of conquest he was converted to Buddhism and filled with remorse for the horrors of war. Future conquests must be "by religion". Like Constantine he called a general council. The canon of Buddhist scriptures was fixed, and many monasteries endowed. Other religions were to be tolerated and assisted. His own son and daughter were sent to convert Ceylon; missionaries also went to Burma, Siam and elsewhere. Edicts were engraved on rocks or pillars in many places. The law was practical, no metaphysical subtilties. It consisted of compassion, liberality, truth, purity, gentleness and saintliness of life, "hearkening to elders, reverence to the aged, and seemly treatment of Brahmins and ascetics, of the poor and wretched, yea, even of slaves and servants". These virtues will bring the only true happiness "in this world and the next".

Why, it is just what is argued here . . . . could he be G's Ashiata Shiemash? It has been vaguely in mind lately that Ashiata did not correspond to any of the religious Founders, was he just G's own ideal? Some things about Ashiata could connect with Asoka, such as the appeal to conscience. Ashiata's marble tablets or inscriptions are mentioned three times. Thirty-five of Asoka's inscriptions have survived, but his very name had been forgotten in India when James Prinsep in 1834 discovered the key to the ancient alphabets on bilingual coins, and was able to start reading the inscriptions. On page 351, in the "*Ashiata*" chapters, G brings in the word "deluge", when a flea sneezes, which could be intended to confirm a connection between the ashokh and Ashiata passages.

If the Flood stories are taken as a parable about continuity, how to preserve something from the flood of time and hand on understanding to future generations, the Ark can be seen as Art or whatever organisation and customs further this, – cave painting, sculpture, myth and story, epics to be learned by heart and publicly recited, inscriptions and books when writing spread.

There is not much record of Asoka's successors; his grandson followed in his footsteps but after that the empire began to break up. However it could be said that through Buddhism Asoka had a long-lasting influence, and the inscriptions have brought his name back into history as one of the few great kings.

Another teasing Indian word is ***sari***, perhaps the world's most graceful if unpractical costume, because it seems to echo saros, the period of 6585 1/3 days used in predicting eclipses of sun or moon. The track of the moon's shadow in successive eclipses of the sun in the same saros series winds round the earth in a spiral rather as the sari is wound round the body.

A similar image is the Mithraic Aion whose lion-headed statues, bearing the keys of heaven, are coiled round by a serpent, typifying the course of the sun on the ecliptic. He was for Mithraism the supreme God, also called Kronos and Zervan Akarana, Boundless Time (Cumont: "***The Mysteries of Mithra***"). But the image could also be a short-hand of the death of Stephen at Leontopolis, while observing an eclipse. Jung's book Aion gives an illustration of such a statue.

22nd July, 1975. An unexpected visit: the landlord had asked an architect friend to look into the possibility of "Turnerising" the roof. He agreed the house wasn't worth such an expensive process, but it was urgent to replace the rotted gutter.

The Pythagoreans and G's many brotherhoods with beautiful names have been in mind lately with the general question of human associations and their ups and downs. Sir Harry Luke in "*An Eastern Chequerboard*" describes a visit in 1913 to Konia, residence of the hereditary successors of Jalau'ddin Rumi (1207–1273) and mainspring of the "great brotherhood which exercises a beneficent influence in the Ottoman empire in the direction of tolerance and breadth of mind, by means of its thousands of lay brothers scattered through every walk of life" – the Mevlevi or Whirling Dervishes. This contrasts with Luke's descriptions of the atmosphere of suspicion in the Sultan's Seraglio at Stamboul, and of the sectarian quarrels of his time in Jerusalem. Miss Merston's account of Benares also gives the impression that holy cities attract evil as well as good.

"*Turn*erising" the roof....ideas about the Goddess Nature and Heaven – too ambitious? Gutter – Gurdjieff. Threads came together as a view of the way G may have seen the future of his Work – not a mass movement, not a new religion, but a brotherhood like the Mevlevi, using the books and movements he provided, to act in society as a leaven, salt, with the aim of preserving quality. "If the salt have lost his savour, wherewith shall it be salted?" (Matt. 5.13).

9. *Michelangelo*

One of the first inexactitudes in art to be noticed was that Michelangelo's Moses has horns. His ark on the Sistine ceiling is not like any ship that ever floated, though it could be a treasure chest. In the Greek flood story Deucalion was saved in a chest which landed on Mount Parnassus, the mountain of Delphi, sacred to Apollo and the Muses and source of the Castalian Spring; this suggests that the story may be symbolic.

Michelanglo seems to have felt an obligation to show full frontal male nudity, except in the drunken Bacchus which is a hermaphrodite. He was attacked for this and even in his lifetime, a pupil was employed to add draperies to the Sistine "Last Judgement". Michelanglo consented, telling Paul IV's messenger: "Let (his Holiness) look to setting the world in order; to reform a picture costs no great trouble".

Gurdjieff also seems to have felt a duty to speak and write of things we would rather not mention, and to draw attention to the lower part of the body. "Flowers are masturbator thing; kitchen garden useful". "Herring is sex-organ – You say God made you, but I say just such sex-organ-herring made you". "Venez manger", to feed the "patron" – tape-worm. It seems that beneath Louis XIV's splendid robes was literally a tape-worm. His doctors' diaries, worthy of Molière's satire, make it probable he had one most of his life (see "Louis XIV" by Louis Bertrand) – part of the price of presiding over that brilliant epoch.

There is a story that during one of G's absences the ladies at the Prieuré worked hard to bring the rose garden into perfect order. They showed him on his return. "Yes, very nice". But later in the day he harnessed the donkey-cart and drove it to and fro in the rose garden, destroying everything; he said the ladies were too much identified. It seems unnecessarily cruel, but the donkey in the rose garden is unforgettable. It is as if G had to create an image of himself as a seed-man, a fecundator, and so he did things that sound outrageous. His ideas were seeds too.

1564 Death of Michelangelo, birth of Shakespeare, One cannot pretend to have studied Shakespeare, but a few points have suggested themselves: his names – Portia, Ophelia, Imogen, Bottom the weaver; Hamlet's discovery that there was someone behind the curtain. In the Tempest, a shipwreck story, Prospero, if it is prosperous, is a bit like fortunate or Faustus, so he might stand for Simon Magus, whose ship may have been wrecked by an ill wind that blew good to the world.

Shakespeare's Antony and Cleopatra follows Plutarch closely, the servant Eros who kills himself rather than his master, the dying Antony hauled up into Cleopatra's "monument". This image of hanging by ropes is haunting: Paul let down from the walls of Damascus, the man sick of the palsy let down through the roof on his bed, Rahab the harlot letting Joshua's spies down from her window in the wall of Jericho. Is it just the hanged man or is it some symbolism of the lines of communication by which the divine powers can act, or be called? One has heard of ''deus ex machina'', machinery presumably involving ropes from which in the Greek plays the gods could appear. Peter Pan flies on wires.

As Michelangelo grew older – he lived to be almost 89 – he ''used the thought of death as the mystagogue of his spirit into the temple of eternal things . . . . and as the means of maintaining self-control and self-coherence amid the ever-shifting illusions of human life''. (The Life by John Addington Symonds, Vol. II p. 311).

Is remembrance of death (*All and Everything* p 1183) a pill for placing restraint on the fluctuations of the mind, for damming the stream to raise its potential? Most of us stop at lesser examples of interrupting the flow to improve attention or build up ''virtue'' in Thring's sense of negative entropy. There has to be a flow of water in the stream, the process will not work when too tired. G gave sensible advice to divide the day, not necessarily in equal proportions, between active-active, active-passive, passive-active, and passive-passive, say a scale from maximum attention to sleep at night. It belongs to ''the art of self-management''.

One can have the wrong sort of ''remembrance of death''. Too much dwelling on funerals, illness and the fate of the body is unnecessarily depressing. It is the hope of new but different life beyond death that one needs to recall.

Ouspensky said we were third-force-blind. It has always rankled because one could not understand, and the blindness is still there; but the idea is also a stimulator, a gadfly like Socrates. All the platitudes and moralisings that have been put in this writing, with a certain feeling of guilt or self-indulgence, that they were not good enough, they were thin, beating one's head against the dichotomies – how can God be both omnipotent and kind, do we have free-will and responsibility or is the future all fore-ordained, permissiveness or prudery, is evil necessary? – all this is one-track thinking, it cannot be resolved on that level.

Did one accept Gurdjieff's Law of Three too easily? Is it

really a legominism for the Trinity, which may itself be a legominism? Other ideas which may have started as legominisms have caused endless argument on the logical level; such are homo-ousios, and the fall of man. About "original sin" it can be said that man does seem capable of much more wickedness than the animals; it is just because he can also climb higher than the animals, his brain does have an extra dimension which gives him more potentiality both for good and ill, for service or cruelty and greed.

In the ***Boolmarshano*** (p 1139) on Good and Evil, G speaks of the Third Force in a more comprehensive way "And as for the third independent World Force, this force is nothing else but only the result of the clash everywhere and in everything of these two fundamental descending and ascending independent forces.

"Although this third independent force is only the result of both first fundamental forces, it is nevertheless the spiritualising and reconciling source of every World formation."

Meanwhile it is already something to see two sides to a question. Years ago Dr. Ratnasuriya from Ceylon quietly stood on his head in the dining room at Coombe Springs to illustrate his point that it was useful to look at things upside down. The economic panacea "growth" may prove disastrous, blessings come all too often "in disguise", boredom can be useful. (May your psyche grow, not your possessions – an idea contributed by the B.B.C. just when this page was under revision).

Beelzebub indeed accuses us of reflecting reality in our attention upside down, and sometimes it is difficult to know which way up to take him, for instance in his defence of polygamy (***A & E*** pp 989–993, 1009); but this is deliberate. His aim was to provoke thought, holding in almost all his tales to two principles (p1165) of which the first is:

> "not to say anything as if it were my own personal opinion, in order that data necessary for your own convictions should not be crystallized in you in a prepared form according to the opinions of another."

Thesis, antithesis, synthesis: perhaps it is all in Hegel, but philosophy is hard to read. Out of the clash of yes and no can come the raising of level to a new understanding. Silence and respect may help the new synthesis to come, the third force, the Holy Immortal. But when one cannot reach the better level, it may be best to hang a warning flag on questions that are too big for everyday thinking, such as the nature of life after death. Symbols are safer. Some day, or in a better state, we shall understand more.

Monday 13th May 1974 – Eureka! A hasty rereading of the chapter **Purgatory** the day before had left the word Surp-Athanatos for the third force, "Holy the Immortal". While dressing, the name of a Hungarian obstetrician heard on a B.B.C. programme trailer came back as worth looking up – correctly it was Semmelweiss. Look under S .... One was sure Surp-Garabed had been met in the encyclopaedia, but how to find it again? Yes, it actually is in the index. The reference is to the article, on the very last page of the volume, on Mush (mentioned in ***R.M.*** p 92) near the upper Euphrates. "Some miles to the west....is the celebrated monastery of Surp Garabed or John the Baptist, an important place of Armenian pilgrimage". It is suggested that this is the same name as Karapet of Tiflis, who pulled the steam whistle to wake the railway workers, in the introductory chapter ***"The Arousing of Thought"***; and that Gurdjieff felt an affinity with the role of John the Baptist, since he called his first published book ***"The Herald of Coming Good"*** .

A pleasing misprint appeared in the New Year 1975 Daily Telegraph magazine; "the order of St. Michael and St. Garage". The connection of George with Gara(bed) is almost a message from him, anyway encouraging.

10. Polly.

Found in a diary hunt, under August 1949, that Mrs. D said about a reading of ***Purgatory:*** "When I died it was direct nearness to God, so wonderful and certain. I know this "babbling streams" of Purgatory is untrue, oriental. How can we work intensively enough to make these bodies, and it can be done". She was very grateful to Mr. Gurdjieff for the idea of the Kesdjan body, which for her explained the Resurrection of Jesus: "It was his Kesdjan body they saw''; but G ''also talks old fashioned nonsense about women'' (May 1949).

Artist, quite unintellectual, Polly, the second Mrs. Bennett, had a gift of saying perceptive things, and a great power of attracting people by her warmth. Though her chosen art was painting, she would have made a consummate actress. We were convinced that she had reached a high level of being through her sacrifices, and stuggles against illnesses, to assist a husband so many years her junior, and that this gave her the force to hold Coombe Springs together. Sometimes one thought of her as Duchess, and we, the household, were her court, closely meshed. Work with her was a training in sensitiveness. Of a girl who had a gyne operation she said: ''If she cannot be an ordinary woman, she shall be an extraordinary one, a saint''.

Glowing in her red silk embroidered dinner dress, under a mass of white curls the result of patient hair-dressing, she was worth devouring with the eyes, for which staring oneself got a merited rebuke. Memory can see her too in a well-worn woollen day dress, big bosom soft for embracing, dainty ankles in silk stockings with cobweb darns, the two-colour gold bracelet dangling on the wrist whose soft skin Dr. Salmanoff praised so enthusiastically, in her pink bedroom with the expensive second-hand curtains – all new textiles were on coupons – and the card table overflowing with correspondence.

Memory has printed a meeting under the big oak tree from the intensive two weeks seminar of 1947. Walking up the path from the spring house one had had such a strong feeling of love for Mrs. B it seemed quite unbearable that soon she would die and we should never meet again. In the light of later theories that feeling is seen as not really personal but fed in from ''somewhere'' to produce a memory-occasion and a clarity, a question for the discussion.

This must be the day. ''Monday 4th August. Fast, with three talks under oak. The right triad of social relationships is rulers, ruled and schools, not oppressors, oppressed and reformers. What could a popular religion, and one for the few, say, that they would listen to? . . . . Duty is the keyword . . . not rights . . .

.. the thought of death has always been a reminder. An explanation of that in terms of eternity might be the new doctrine''. The concluding chord of the seminar was that we should live as children of the New Epoch, whose master idea would be mutuality, as that of the Epoch now reaching its end had been the sacredness of the individual.

A question from the earlier week: ''What is the difference between suffering and negativeness?'' ''When suffering is taken wrongly''. Could it be said separating negativeness from suffering is soul-making work and this is why the Institutes had to put people under such pressure? ''Do you think you're the only person with a sorrow?'' asked Mrs. B once.

Mrs. B's scoldings were method. ''Did you see how Mrs. – took her scolding yesterday, neither tears nor angry nor rude? That is a big step forward''. This housemaid would accept the scolding and believe she *was* awful and then get black rebellious moods. Eventually she came to see it might not be her, there might be injustice in the outer world, the self-blame, worrying about self was in any case useless. But one still had to find an answer to one's own problems.

On a lighter note – May 1949 ''Mrs. B gets Edith to have her hair permed and in curls, great success''. Edith, a newcomer, was teased about her ironmongery–hairpins. She was German and had been working at Barnardo's. She must have had proud parents to give her such a mouthful of names – Edith Ottilie Nanny Margarethe Wichmann – anagram WOMEN. She took a big share in nursing Mrs. B's last years and then became a leading Subud ''helper''.

Instructive rows from Mr. B have returned to mind – for misunderstandings one would now accuse ''the spirits'' of having plotted. One was for growing crocuses in a silver copy of the Vaphio cup. ''But it is my own, mayn't I do what I like with my own?'' It was a legacy from an uncle-godfather. It turned out Mr. B had a copy too, produced by a more accurate method, and thought his had been used. In such ways one learned to have more respect for silver and antiques, in spite of talk about non-attachment. The two Vaphio gold cups, found in

S. Greece in 1889, date from maybe 1500 B.C. and show the trapping of wild bulls by rope, net or a decoy tame cow. The Bennetts had taught us about the symbolism of the Chinese ox-herding pictures. May not these early bull-fighting sports and art also have had a teaching element, the taming of man's wild nature?

Non-attachment should not excuse carelessness. Perhaps the aim is love without losing yourself, with people as with things, two-ended arrow. Love conscience more. Grabbing or stealing cannot be a good way to start a relationship aiming at marriage, nor does the spectator feel 'managing' him by feeding the tape-worm vanity, by excessive flirtation, or by ordinary nagging, can be good. Honour to the men who wear wedding rings, so you know they are not available. But people who are allowed the happiness of a well-balanced marriage seem to be sent misfortunes to face together.

"Love of consciousness evokes the same in response
Love of feeling evokes the opposite
Love of body depends only on type and polarity".

(*A & E* p 361). In his defence of polygamy Gurdjieff's young Persian says monogamy is, as a rule, possessive (*A & E* p 992). Touché. Pride did not want to be one of a harem. Only love of consciousness can surmount that.

From school days one had had a tendency sometimes to make unfortunate remarks, such as "Why are you kicking me under the table?" Evidently for saying something "tactless", a word whose meaning one had not yet learnt. At Coombe at the Bennetts' breakfast there was a shocked rebuke from Mr. B for a reference to scrubbing the back passage. (In the early days we did a good deal of scrubbing bare wooden floors; there is a skill to be learned to do it effectively and not just smear mud.) At first one could not understand what was wrong and Mr. B accepted that it had been said in innocence of any double meaning. A lesson in symbolism.

Prince Philip once joked about his tendency to "dontopedalogy" opening his mouth and putting his foot in it, so others may have this unfortunate gift for saying the wrong thing. Mrs. B dropped on some tactless remark that slipped out to her, with whom one did try to be alert. "But what made you say it?" Housemaid had been asking herself that. "Sorry, Mrs. B. I just didn't have enough attention to keep a watch on what I was saying".

"Is it possible, really, to remember oneself while speaking?" All this one has been able to do is to catch the echo of the tone of voice; if it is rising querulously it is a warning to draw back. The Reader's Digest had a joke about the talkative woman told to think before she spoke: "But how can I know what I think till I hear myself saying it?" A group member W.W.D. once said ruefully: "It is rather a mess the way we speak". It does seem as if having done what one can, for much of the time one must trust habit and the unconscious to look after what comes out. Hygiene of thoughts is one precaution.

21st October 1974: get out the bundle of old folders for re-use. "Here's a nice clean one. Whose is it?" Madame Heliane's. So one had better put in another merited rebuke found in diary. Mr. B "I was horrified to hear that you didn't want Mme Heliane to play for the movements yesterday. You know how you curl up at the least suggestion that you're not wanted. Other people are just the same", How indeed could one have been so callous? That there is now no recollection at all of the incident says that it happened in "sleep". Truth to tell it cannot have been long before the time when Edith replaced Madame Heliane as movements pianist; perhaps old age was really catching up with her. Madame Heliane was Mrs. Bennett's sister, a former opera singer, teacher of singing and elocution, and accompanist of Caruso. She played devotedly for movements for years and showed particular kindness to this writer. It was accidentally finding a little old book given by her: "Oriental Poems" by Sir Edwin Arnold, selected by J.M. Watkins, 1904, which opened one's eyes to an interesting possibility about the Katha Upanishad and Nachiketas' sacrifice and dialogue with Death.

One day Mrs. B was delivering a scolding that was felt to be unfair; "Why sit there and be abused?"; yet she was ill and one loved her and feared to harm her by answering back.

Trapped, doublebind. Presently one got up and walked out without a word. It was the last time; some lesson had been learned, perhaps independence. Puzzling is that one now connects it with another walk-out from that room, from an impossible Council meeting in 1959 which exceptionally was held there and not in the study; and that was the end of being anything but nominally Council Secretary, another good-bye.

In an illness of Mrs. B's there had been a poignant realisation that the only way one could help was by staying away. When she died in 1958, after four years of near-blindness and a dementia in which she still said oddly appropriate things, ex-housemaid did not learn of her death for 24 hours, having felt so low the day before, that, somewhat withdrawn, she did not notice anything unusual; and all she could say on being told was "It's no use pretending one hasn't been longing for it to happen". She had put up a defensive barrier.

The relationship sometimes resembled an earlier one with Great Aunt Ella, who did so much for the education and art training of a motherless child, yet encouraged personality problems by her emotional demands and perhaps gave a fear of sex from her own failed marriage. Only at 40, after her world turned upside down, were this rabbit's negativenesses and unfulfilled promise and hypochondria gradually explained as preparing for a withdrawal from life for a special purpose, a summons from the unconscious to its compulsions and maxi-daydreams. "God" can be Hera – stepmother, tormenting his creatures to teach them toughness and discrimination among the negative moods.

Diary rereading shows that memory has over stressed the bad times in the early years at Coombe. Why were Sundays so wonderful and Mondays so awful? Now it is seen as natural reaction, emotional fatigue. "I could lift you up to heaven, but you could not stay there", Mr. Gurdjieff is reported to have said. Mondays have to be endured. Coombe was a forcing house.

This preacher of pious remembering of the dead can feel affection for many of them and yet does not do so for the Aunt who was so close and was in many ways a fine character. There is only a small sense of guilt about the exclusion, which is held to be because of the special role she had to play in this relationship. Is there a distinction between the individual being and the roles he/she is called upon to play? When the play is over will all be forgiven?

With actual stepmother there was not personal involvement; one was grateful for her housekeeping and that she went on remembering birthdays; her much repainted tray is still the bedside table. She had an unusual name, Syria, chosen by her godfather Dr. Barnardo. One tried to do one's outer duty to her, but there was an inner barrier justified because of her will to dominate her own children. When she died in 1968 there was some feeling of guilt, should one have tried harder, until an odd sophistry appeared – that this rejection might even help her to slough off in "Purgatory" what was hardened wrongly in her nature. There is an upside down passage in Mr. G's Third Series, about remembering the faults of the deceased, which might suggest something of the sort.

Why didn't they use a more experienced person for this writing, and not an old maid who feels like a celibate pope drafting bulls on birth control! She remembers saying: "She's got husband trouble", presumably of someone asking to see Mrs. B for advice, and then feeling shame, was it callous from a spinster? "No, perfectly correct". Of course there is wife-trouble too. Seen from outside, marriage sometimes looks frightening. Perhaps one still has the fairy-tale notion that people will marry and "live happy ever after"; but there must come times of reaction, "breaks in the octave".

The one-sided Catholic rules for marriages of mixed religion can't be a good basis for equal partnership; nor the Catholic tendency to burden a marriage with too many children. One wants to see marriage as aiming at "love of consciousness", a relation of kinship, family, essence, joint work and aim, and not only "love of body", though recognising this is necessary and strong in young people, since they have to do Nature's work of continuing the race. On an idealistic view, sexual attraction may be seen as an indication that this person is your fate, this is how "marriages are made in heaven"; then it is not something to be used lightly for kicks or variety, or for advertising cigarettes and drinks. But life is not ideal. The art is to make something with the materials available.

11. The Fairy Tales

Why wasn't the second principle of Beelzebub's method in telling his tales quoted in the section on Michelangelo? Because of inability to construe the twelve line sentence. Mme de Salzmann (salt-man) is reported to have said the text is sometimes defective, Mr. Gurdjieff would not wait for a full revision. But the words "Premeditated and selected sequence" ring a bell, and provide a lead to a subject one has somehow been prevented from expanding into before.

In these experiences the **order** in which the material has appeared has been important. One example was a bargain offer complete translation of Grimm's Fairy Tales (Routledge and Kegan Paul) fifteen shillings, at a time when mind was ready to feel richness of meaning in them, but could not have taken in more adult works. They were read and reread to the child-visitors in 1959–61, Bennett brothers and Pianoff sisters, whose ages fitted like one family. Only Katie was really too young and would never choose anything but the Wolf and the Seven Little Kids, a first class junior story with its dialogue repetitions, a sex-warning of the danger of letting the wolf in, the birth, and resurrection, theme of the youngest kid hiding in the clock-case, and of the others being cut out alive from the wolf's tummy; and as it is about animals, not humans, it is less likely to cause nightmares.

In "The Six Servants" a marriage task is: "You shall fetch me my ring which I have dropped into the Red Sea". In "The King's Son who Feared Nothing" the giant blinded the King's son and led him to the top of a precipice, hoping he would fall and be killed, so that the giant could take a ring from him. But the faithful lion pushed the giant over the precipice and drew his master back, leading him to a brook whose water restored his sight. It was strong meat to a mind shocked by the death of a friend by a fall; every ripe chestnut which fell through the trees behind the Fishbowl that October brought a shiver of horror.

There are no lions in the gospels but there is the idea of height and of falling. In Matthew's version of the temptation of Jesus. after the forty days fast and the temptation to change stones into bread, the devil invited him to cast himself down from a pinnacle of the temple, and again on the exceeding high mountain he said, "All these things will I give thee, if thou wilt fall down and worship me". In Acts 20 there is a rather gratuitous miracle of the restoration of Eutychus, who went to sleep during Paul's long preaching in an upper chamber, and fell out of a window "from the third loft". He was taken up dead, but recovered after Paul said the life was still in him.

Fairy tales often use three-fold repetition. In Acts the story of Paul's conversion is repeated three times, first in chapter 9 and then in his speeches in chapters 22 and 26, though "it is hard for thee to kick against the pricks" only occurs twice.

Another favourite book was "Medieval Stories" translated from the Swedish, London, Sands and Co. , 1902 – illustrated by W. Heath Robinson. It was among the books left by a "cousin" killed in the first world war; others were a school prize – Kingsley's "Heroes", and a bound volume of the Boy's Own Paper with a serial about a space ship. One of the medieval stories is about Charlemagne having a repeated dream in which an angel bade him go out and steal with a master thief Alegast. This led to the king overhearing a conspiracy against himself. One has met a number of stories about successful thieves; they always arouse a feeling that the two thieves crucified with Jesus have some secret meaning. The stories of Karl the Great and his twelve paladins, and of Arthur with his knights of the round table sound as if they owed something to the example of Jesus with his disciples. The Holy Grail suggests that there is a mystery to be sought.

"The Juniper Tree," beginning "It is now long ago, quite two thousand years", is a beautiful story in Grimm's which is hardly suitable for children. The killing of a son by a stepmother who cooks him for the father to eat, and the changing into a bird, belong to Greek mythology, but the sister who gathers the bones into a silk handkerchief, the bird dropping a millstone round the stepmother's neck, and the restoration of the boy seem Christian themes. Children do eat **us** by their continual demands.

The sister, little Marlinchen, leads to fantasies one had about Mary Magdalene. When the mind was first mad it was full of ideas about "The Woman" – goddess, or the Unconscious, or that Jesus must have had a relation with a woman. It was fancied that like Buddha he was a young-husband (Sir Francis Younghusband, name of the leader of the British expedition into Tibet) who deserted a wife and son in order to pursue his spiritual mission, and that Mary Magdalene might have been his wife or girl friend, and mother of Mark.

In his chapter "***Religion***", Gurdjieff turns the role of Judas upside down. He is reported to have told Mr. Bennett that Judas and Pavel (Paul) were the two best friends Jesus had, and to have charged Mr. Bennett to give a lecture about Judas. So one pondered over Judas, being driven to turn to the distant past to escape the unpleasant present.

> Only God could play the role of Judas.
> The Devil is God in disguise.
> Then must the Devil always win?
> No, it is our business to wrestle with him.

If there is positive inspiration, perhaps there also has to be negative inspiration, that is: temptation and dementia. Some children slow at lessons show remarkable guile in the battle with grown-ups. Maybe the devil is acting through them – but one trusts they will not grow up into agents of the devil, criminals. When temptation comes it is too late, resistance is absent unless you are forewarned by sensible upbringing, or resolved, by repentance and change of attitude, not to be caught next time.

A climax was reached early in 1961 during a menstrual period, a time when there always seemed a lot of wildness and magic about. One fancied that Judas might have stolen away the body of Jesus, under cover of a rain-storm, and that the disciples literally ate it to preserve it from his enemies.

This was really going too far and was perhaps the turning

point leading to seeing these fancies were getting nowhere and there never could have been a divine person like Jesus, things don't happen like that. It must have been Mrs. B who told a story about a ''miraculée'', healed in the train returning from Lourdes, who later began complaining that ''le bon dieu'' might also have given her money and a husband. Eventually her disease returned, but now she had lost her faith and her good attitudes. Miracles aren't really good for people.

Resentment against deception by the churches continued a long time. It is not surprising they had to lay so much stress on the virtue of faith, or that so many people (like Jung's father) had to suffer torments of doubt. One supposes some won through to a deeper understanding, some left or kept quiet, but how many had to compromise and become hollow, preaching what they could not feel?

A first approach to new ideas about ''what really happened'' had already come in September, 1960. A child called Catherine, normally amenable, had behaved in a really extraordinary manner and led to the idea that Catherine of Alexandria ''was'' Mary Magdalene. Then how did she get to Alexandria?

In 1961 we had a four year old Aaron who was always going round Coombe calling ''has anybody seen my Steve?'' (his father). It eventually suggested that the central death, round which the gospel crystallised, was that of a Stephen, really so named, the first martyr, or witness to faith in the life after death and the rule of heaven, with his festival nearest to Christmas, on Boxing day; and that there was a significant relationship, whatever its nature or degree of frustration of physical consumation, between Stephen and Catherine.

Both names are found rather frequently in literature. A Victorian story set in Greece gave a clue: Amaryllis, T. Fisher Unwin, M DCCC XCI, bookplate Dudley Hervey; Pseudonym Library with the author's name printed in Greek capitals. The only footnote says: ''A play on his name Stephen – Stephanos – a crown or wreath'', and the text has ''Well – yesterday – you were a crown of thorns?''

* * * * * * *

12. Jung

Carl Gustav Jung's "*Memories, Dreams, Reflections*" gives precious indications of the inner experience of someone who had a special relationship with "the Unconscious" from early childhood. With dates 1875 – 1961 he is a close contemporary of Gurdjieff's, and there might have been some similarity in their development. Both mention interest in table-turning and spiritualism; and refer to selling antiques.

Jung has his first memorable dream (of a phallus in an underground temple) at three or four years old, but it was years, even decades, before he understood it fully. In his student days he hesitated to read Nietzsche from a fear that he might be like Nietzsche "at least in regard to the 'secret' which had isolated him from his environment". When Jung did read Nietzsche, it was a tremendous experience, yet Zarathustra was morbid. Jung reflected "Nietzsche had discovered his No. 2 only late in life, when he was already past middle age, wheras I had known mine ever since boyhood. Nietzsche had spoken naively and incautiously about this arrheton, thing not to be named, as though it were quite in order. But I had noticed in time that this only leads to trouble". (p 123 Fontana paperback edition).

A fruitful time was Jung's "confrontation with the unconscious" beginning in 1912 and into the World War. He speaks of the "unswerving conviction" that he was obeying a higher will. The writing of "Seven Sermons to the Dead" in 1916 "began with a restlessness, but I did not know what it meant, or what 'they' wanted of me ... the door-bell rang frantically, no one was there. The whole house was as if crammed full of spirits. 'What in the world is this?' Then they cried out in chorus, 'We have come back from Jerusalem where we found not what we sought'." That is the beginning of the Septem sermones, described as written by Basilides in Alexandria (pp 215–6). "The soul, the anima, establishes the relationship to the unconscious. In a certain sense this is also a relationship to the collectivity of the dead; for the unconscious corresponds to the mythic land of the dead, the land of the ancestors" (p 216).

"I was going about laden with thoughts of which I could speak to no one: they would only have been misunderstood. I felt the gulf between the external world and the interior world of images, in its most painful form. I could not yet see that interaction of both worlds which I now understand" (p 219).

It is "a grave mistake to think that it is enough to gain some understanding of the images and that knowledge can here make a halt. Insight into them must be converted into an ethical obligation. Not to do so is to fall prey to the power principle, and this produces dangerous effects which are destructive not only to others but even to the knower. The images of the unconscious place a great responsibility upon a man" (p 218). This is one way of answering the question of Hasnamuss responsibility.

In Jung's Liverpool dream (1927) it was foggy, dark and raining, but in the centre of the radially laid-out city was a round pool with a small island, and on it a blossoming magnolia in a blaze of sunlight. The dream was the outcome of his mandala drawings. The goal of development is the self. "There is no linear evolution, there is only a circumambulation of the self". In the blackness of life he had had a vision of unearthly beauty at the centre. (p 222–4)

Trouble in spelling Nietzsche caused reference to the encyclopaedia. His dates were 1844 – 1900. His father, a pastor like Jung's, died prematurely from a fall down a flight of steps. A little book by A.R. Orage, "Nietzsche in Outline and Aphorism" 1907, says he was of Polish descent. **Nyet** is Russian for No, and he was a denying force, "a destructive genius of the first order" (Encyclopaedia).

After an exceptionally productive year in 1888 Nietzsche became insane and never recovered. Though the encyclopaedia is too too polite to mention it, the cause of the twelve years' insanity is reported to be the terrifying V.D. or S.T.D. (sexually transmitted disease) syphilis. Promiscuity is horrible. The researches and hygienic campaigns of recent generations have taken the fear out of tuberculosis, smallpox, syphilis and other diseases, but if impunity makes us careless these troubles may come back. There is talk of strains resistant to antibiotics. We shall not like it if rabies returns to this country. Even nits in the hair are reported again, and worse, something very like the White Slave Trade.

The Nietzsche article by Oscar Levy, M.D., L.R.C.P., M.R.C.S. speaks of the gospel of the superman and the eternal recurrence, master morality, will to power, aristocratic doctrine, topsy-turvy world, and unwanted disciples indulging their ''chaotic instincts beyond good and evil''. Emancipation of woman will lead to loss of her charm, and to defective offspring. ''His psychological ruthlessness tore veil after veil from ideals cherished for centuries." His ideas evidently proved stimulating; he seems to have been both right and wrong.

In his chapter on the Superman (or Hero) Ouspensky in ''*The New Model of the Universe*'' quotes Nietzsche, ''Man is a rope over an abyss . . . .What is great in man is that he is a bridge and not a goal''. ''What falleth, that shall one also push''.

Association brings up another bridge metaphor, from Akbar's inscription on the triumphal arch (1602) at his soon-deserted city of Fatehpur Sikri: ''Jesus said: the world is a bridge, pass over it but do not build houses on it''. ''A'' seems to be a good initial for Kings: Alexander, Asoka, Augustus, Arthur, Alfred, Akbar. It is also a good letter for beginning and ending continents, with the exception of Europe.

13. The Orthodox Eastern Churches

The paragraph about Mme de Beausobré in ''Goodness'' seemed irrelevant when it arose, but now relevance has appeared. Both her lectures on ''Persistent Trends in Eastern Christianity'' (*Systematics,* June 1969) and ''*A Treasury of Russian Spirituality*'' by G. P. Fedotov, Sheed and Ward, 1950, speak of Kenoticism, in the sense of charitable humility as well as of non-resistance, or voluntary suffering, being the typical motif of Russian Christianity. If this is not the source of the second part of Gurdjieff's so often repeated prescription of conscious labour and intentional suffering, it is at least closely related to the idea.

The new red Chambers dictionary gives Kenosis – Greek, emptying, and a reference to Philippians 2. Verses 3–8 read:

"Let nothing be done through strife or vainglory; but in lowliness of mind let each esteem other better than themselves. Look not every man on his own things, but every man also on the things of others.
Let this mind be in you, which was also in Christ Jesus: Who, being in the form of God, thought it not robbery to be equal with God: But made himself of no reputation, and took upon him the form of a servant, and was made in the likeness of men: And being found in fashion as a man, he humbled himself, and became obedient unto death, even the death of the cross."

Verse 4 recalls "the ninth commandment of our CREATOR, namely: 'Do unto another's as you would do unto your own'" (*A & E* p 93), which had seemed a slightly surprising version of the golden rule.

Fedotov tells of Father Alexander **Yelchaninov**, born 1881, died 1934 in Paris, whose life has a few points of resemblance with G's *A*bram ***Yelov***. Yelchaninov came of a military family; he studied history and philology at St. Petersburg University. At the time of the first revolution in Russia 1905–6 he and a few friends tried to enter politics as an underground group called the "Christian Brotherhood of Struggle". Later they, like most of the religious intelligentsia, became conservative or national-spirited. Yelchaninov spent the last years of the old regime as a teacher and headmaster in a progressive high school in Tiflis. He was "alive and well" after the revolution, but in the south of France.

G says that his friend Yelov had wanted to enter the army cadet school; later he became a great linguist and received a degree in philology. Supposing G did intend to connect Yelchaninov with his Yelov (originally construed Abraham Yahweh – lover), what would be the point? To show that he did value his Orthodox Church? The idea mentioned in ***"A bit more comparative religion"*** that the plaster casts in the Yelov chapter represent the soldier of Pompeii who was "faithful unto death" can be made to connect with Christ's being "obedient unto death" in the verse just quoted.

There is also Vladimir Soloviev, 1853 – 1900, philosopher, and inspirer of symbolist poets, and influenced by Dostoievski. His father was a historian, Rector of Moscow University. Vladimir studied theology and philosophy, but his criticism of the government earned him his dismissal from university lectureships. One of his books was called "***War, Progress and the End of History, including a short story of the Anti-Christ***" (1900).

He dwells specially on "the theandric mystery; god-manhood – as distinct from supermanhood – which can be attained by man only because God became man and to which no personal, human 'merit' can therefore be attached". His second theme sounds rather Gnostic, the Sophianic mystery, the Wisdom Angel as the Throne of the Trinity, or the Essential Fourth, connected with the Mother of Jesus.

Looking through G's section on Soloviev in ***Remarkable Men,*** some points can be inverted to correspond with this Vladimir – such as being his mother's favourite for the Sophiology, drinking for inspiration, and begging your pardon, the counterfeit notes could be theology. So it may be G did take the name from him.

It seems possible that in some aspects the Eastern Churches have remained closer to the original Christianity, as ritual and symbol, not history. What a lovely moment it is at the annual memorial services on October 29th when the flame is passed into the congregation, each kindling his candle from his neighbour's. Mme de Beausobré says that the Eastern Church particularly values St. John's gospel. She describes the discipline for the laity as gathered round the event of Cana of Galilee, striving, by a multitude of small decisions, to turn into wine the muddy water of life in society and in the family. It is somewhat like G's Fourth Way.

From a distance one cannot see that the Greek church has much moral or ethical influence on public life in Greece or Cyprus today. It has been said that the English speaking countries are living on an inheritance of Protestant ethics, now fast fading. Can we not do something to restore the ethical quest?

14. *European Philosophers*

2–3 October 1974. "Don't philosophise". Finding philosophy too hard to read this person tends to condemn it as mere juggling with words, and a means of "hiding these things from the wise and prudent" (Matt. 11.25). Of course this won't do. It is mental training. You must start from some set of ideas about the world and the purpose of living, in a language appropriate to current education; and there would appear to be legominisms in philosophy too.

The chain of modern philosophy has been part of the battle for freedom of the mind. Now we are in danger of having the tyranny of a new orthodoxy and dogmatism – Marxism – fastened on us, without the self-correcting elements of the old.

Bad news. General Spinola has resigned in Portugal rather than be a puppet of leftist Young Officers. As so often, the first leader of moderate reform is swept aside by more violent revolution. Perhaps it is not accident that the name Spinola resembles Spinoza (1632 – 1677) whose parents, Portuguese crypto-Jews, fled to Holland to find religious freedom. He was educated in Hebrew at the Jewish school, and learned the beginnings of his biblical criticism from earlier Jewish writers. "In the biblical commentary by Abraham Ibn Ezra (1092–1167) one meets with many 'a word to the wise' directing attention to some inconsistency in Scripture, to the post-Mosaic authorship of parts at least of the so-called 'Five Books of Moses', or to the different author ship of the two parts of Isaiah." (Abraham Wolf, Encyclopaedia).

At 23 Spinoza was excommunicated by the Jewish authorities, but Christians, particularly a sect called Collegiants or Mennonites, sought him as a Hebrew teacher. "His age was remarkably lacking in historical sense . . . .saintly contemporaries like John Bunyan and Manasseh ben Israel made the most fantastic use of scripture text, while militant clerics, relying on the ignorant bibliolatry of the masses, misapplied Bible texts to gain their ends."

For fear of the Calvinists, very little of Spinoza's philosophy could be published till after his death, from consumption brought on by the glass dust of his lens polishing. He was only 44.

The encyclopaedia sketches his ethics and says he did not teach asceticism. ''Circumstances compelled him to be extremely frugal and live on a few pence a day,'' but he urged that ''it is part of a wise man to use the world and delight himself in it as best he may, though not to satiety, for that is no delight.'' We may picture him received by his protectors in bourgeois interiors like those painted by Vermeer, who had almost the same life-span – 1632 – 75.

Spinoza distinguishes three ascending grades of knowledge: opinion, reason and intuition. Opinion is pre-scientific. Reason sees the scientific connections of things, but it is imperfect because rather abstract. It reveals the course of single threads, ''world-lines'', in the fabric of reality, not the whole pattern. Intuitive knowledge (G's Understanding?) is only possible for a mind that has been through the discipline of the rational stage.

One who tends to confuse names with the same initial has had difficulty separating Leibnitz and Lessing. Leibnitz, 1646–1716, contemporary and rival of Newton, visited Spinoza at the Hague. He was a precocious scholar ''with a wonderful power of rapid and continuous work. Even when travelling his time was employed in solving mathematical problems''. Did he invent the word theodicy (dike-justice)? The saying ''everything is for the best in the best of all possible worlds'' originates in his Théodicée. He tried to reconcile this optimism with the existence of evil, but the problem of evil and suffering leads beyond logical thinking.

Gurdjieff's friend Pogossian ''was always working at something, because he was convinced no conscious work was ever wasted, and hoped to teach his nature not to be lazy.'' (*R.M.* p 107 and p 117).

Lessing 1729 – 1781, dramatist and critic, is not strictly a philosopher, but is something of a hero. For about a century, though Spinoza's writings were studied and his ideas borrowed his name was anathema. Lessing, and then Goethe and Coleridge, did most to rehabilitate him. Lessing's own life was full of difficulties and disappointments. At the end of the Seven Years War in 1763 he resumed interrupted studies: he ''investigated the early history of Christianity and penetrated more deeply than any contemporary thinker into the significance of Spinoza's philosophy''. For the last part of his life he was librarian at Wolfenbüttel to the Prince of Brunswick, a post earlier held by Leibniz.

He was shown a manuscript: ''An Apology or Defence for the Rational Worshippers of God''by H. S. Reimarus, a pastor at Hamburg. He took the bold step of publishing parts as ''Fragments of an Unknown Author'', suggesting they might be the work of a deist and heretic, J. L. Schmidt, who was safely dead. Lessing implied he did not agree with these views but that the author had a right to express them. One attacked the account of the Israelite crossing of the Red Sea; another said the Resurrection story was fabricated by Jesus' disciples to save them from returning to manual work. ''In reality Christianity is founded on a gigantic fraud but few have noticed the credibility gap'' (from a review of a translation of Reimarus' ''Fragments'') – or rather those who saw it were not ''allowed'' to speak of it except in hints. How did the deception arise? Was it a necessary part of the historical plan or was a mistake made somewhere? Unanswerable question. Let him who is without sin cast the first stone.

In ***All and Everything*** (p 82 – 89) Gurdjieff tells how the comet Kondoor collided with planet Earth as a result of erroneous calculations by a certain Sacred Individual. The Moon and another fragment, now forgotten but called by the Atlanteans ''Anulios'' or ''Kimespai'', ''Never-Allowing-One-to Sleep-in-Peace'', were broken off. To prevent further disasters a Most High Commission with the help of the Angel Looisos provisionally implanted the maleficent organ Kundabuffer at the base of the spinal column of the three-brained beings of planet Earth, causing them to perceive reality topsy-turvy.

It seems possible G did see his mission as connected with a sort of Second Coming, which would try to produce a corrective to erroneous calculations. This is the question we do have to ask: what is needed now? The world seems desperately to need more honest thinking and speaking, but just how? G said there is stupid sincerity and clever sincerity, stupid insincerity and clever insincerity. Guidance for the next step we must ask.

The Wolfenbüttel Fragments were bitterly attacked. Finally, in deference to the consistory the Brunswick Government confiscated them and ordered Lessing to discontinue the controversy, so he returned to "his old pulpit, the stage". He wrote "Nathan the Wise" to show that noble character may be associated with the most diverse creeds. One of his last writings, nominally about freemasonry, was "to plead for a humane and charitable spirit in opposition to a narrow patriotism, an extravagant respect for rank and exclusive devotion to any particular church". The enemies are different now, but we still need to defend that humane and charitable spirit against those who would impose a new intolerance. Lessing "was succeeeded by poets and philosophers who gave Germany for a time the first place in the intellectual life of the world, and it was Lessing, as they themselves acknowledged, who prepared the way for their achievements" (encyc.).

The long-lived Kant (1724 – 1804) at Königsberg also excited the oppostion of the adherents of historical Christianity, and was obliged by his King to promise to avoid religious subjects from 1793 till 1797, when the King died; fear of the French Revolution played a part in this ban.

Fichte (1762 – 1814) influenced by Kant, was a professor of philosophy at Jena from 1793 to 1799, its most brilliant period. A paper in which he defined God as the moral order of the Universe led to a cry of atheism, and his resignation. From 1810-12 he was rector of the new Berlin University.

Plutarch in "Isis and Osiris" says (Loeb p 157); "others while they fly from superstition as from a quagmire, on the other hand unwittingly fall, as it were, over a precipice into atheism". The mind's demand for freedom from the theologians can turn into "freethinking" and materialism, throwing out the baby with the bath water. The "Hegelian Left" leads to Karl Marx and he towards violent revolution, a great deal of suffering, and new masters not much better than the old. The problem of death is still shelved, and psychology becomes the science of brain washing and manipulation. If only the materialist West could renew its sense of real values before all personal freedom is lost!

You cannot make people good by passing laws, nor by shutting criminals up in prison together. Laws can only enforce minimum requirements on the worst cases. The general sense of values is influenced by television and other entertainment, newspapers, schools and universities, but are they leading us in the right direction?

15. *Defective Thinking*

The study under Mr. Ouspensky of the "hindrances", above all negative emotions (C. S. Nott's explanation of them is excellent) but also day-dreaming, lying, justifying, imaginary activity, unnecessary talking, and all the work against Madame Vanity and Mr. Self-love, were very valuable – though too much emphasis can be placed on the negative side. There was not enough positive hope because the goal was unattainable. The conclusion from O's experiments was humility because you could not carry them out. Mr. Gurdjieff was able to give you so much determination that you were able to continue doing his tasks, and so acquire self-discipline.

"When I am connected with outside, I live . . . .We have only one place for our psychic experiences." Wounded self-love fills that place and closes all the doors for a long time.(Views from the Real World p 276). Self-satisfaction, admiring oneself, can also fill that centre of attention and cut one off from outside. This must be why the religions seek humility; the right kind of humility makes clean and open – but also vulnerable, Mr. G implies on p 275. "True self-love – which unfortunately we do not possess – is desirable . . . . . .and proves that a given man is a particle of heaven." (p 277). One should in general be too proud to steal or to accept bribes.

One of Ouspensky's most useful contributions is now seen as his definition of different qualities of thinking, in the preface to the second edition (1934) of "***A New Model of the Universe***". He distinguishes four levels; Higher Mind with esoteric knowledge, Psychological Mind, Logical Mind and Defective Mind. Spinoza's ascending scale of opinion, reason, intuition has the same idea of different qualities.

Ordinary "logical" thinking is sufficient for everyday life, but it becomes "defective" when it tries to deal with questions that are too big for it. Metrication, spelling reforms, superstitions and false theories are given as examples of defective thinking. (However in fact it would seem that every day life is looked after more by the practical, moving-centre, spatially-orientated "right brain" than by the logical, verbal "left brain".)

"A logical mind which knows its limitedness and is strong enough to withstand the temptation to venture into problems beyond its powers and capacities becomes a 'psychological mind'. The psychological method is much more difficult, and disappointing, because by following it "a man often sees he does not understand anything and does not know what to do. Whereas by following the logical method he always understands everything and always knows what to do".

"... a man of logical mind cannot see that Soviet Russia is a plague-house". One thought Ouspensky, as an exile, might be prejudiced. But the Soviets have exported a great deal more plague since 1934.

O quotes Ibsen on ageing truths (which have become defective): ".... there is not much nourishment in such food .... All the truths belonging to the majority are like ancient rancid bacon or like rotten green ham; and from them comes all the moral scurvy which is eating itself into the life of the people around us."

A few points from the article on Ibsen (1828 – 1906): one of his main ideas was the supreme importance of individual character; in the development of the individual he saw the only hope a really cultured and enlightened society. He was disappointed by the reform movements because they all tended to subordinate the individual to the state, and for Ibsen the state, the great compact majority, was always the enemy. His interpreters, like Shaw, were mostly sentimental rationalists, who saw "that the dramatist waged an unceasing war against conventional Christianity, but failed to observe that he did so, not under the banner of rationalism, but in the name of an intenser Christianity".

Defective thinking does really seem to be contagious and to be an inherent weakness of the human mind. We have such short memory as well as short fore-sight. We forget how many of our present troubles may be attributed to quite recent political "remedies": abolition of the death penalty, taxpayers' subsidy of trade union strike funds via public assistance, pressure for impossible equality in, and state monopoly of,schooling, over-rapid expansion of universities, too many demands on the welfare state which is becoming bankrupt, appeasement of terrorists. On the other side one sees financial interests simply out to mke a lot of money, asset-strippers, developers putting up hideous and sometimes unwanted skyscrapers ("What happens if they have to come down?" asked the demolition man) just as a speculation, introduction of television advertisement by a public relations pressure campaign, legalisation of more gambling, "the politics of prosperity" and growth-at-all-costs and inflation, unnecessary administrative reorganisations and increasing bureaucracy.

Here is something: Walter Bagehot (1826 – 1877) quoted by W.F. Deedes in the "Daily Telegraph", (11.10.74), "Most men catch the words that are in the air, and the rhythm which comes to them, they do not know from whence; an unconscious imitation determines their words and makes them say what of themselves they would never have thought of saying". Is that why defective thinking spreads, just as intellectual fashion, trendiness? Then it *is* caused by what Gurdjieff calls our criminal essence-suggestibility; it had seemed an exaggerated diagnosis.

One of G's surprises is that Beelzebub earned his reward, the regrowth of his horns, by ***impartial mentation.*** So thinking does matter. One feels defective thinking is not only stupidity. It is often driven by emotions that have not been examined honestly. "Freethinkers" of various sorts are, one suspects, often unconsciously seeking to justify indulgence of their own animal urges. In the heat of politics it is natural enough to look for arguments supporting one's own interests: power-seeking masquerades as idealism and progress, deliberately manipulating people's hopes and fears and hates, using the good words to turn truth back to front or inside-out like a glove, in Orwell's double-think.

In the introduction to his Selections from Plato (1940), Livingstone writes of "our normal practice of using words without a precise idea of their meaning. If Socrates was alive today, he would be asking our politicians, journalists and others what exactly they meant by liberty or democracy or a classless society, or by any other slogan or catch word of the moment." However a logical definition of democracy, say as rule by majority vote, is not enough; it is how historical democracies have worked, the particular weaknesses they are liable to in contrast with other systems, that must be studied.

Our Church is ill. When what should be the guardian of truthfulness itself supports a lie, demanding faith in the historicity of its Saviour and supressing inconvenient books and people, is it then any wonder that the Apostles of Revolution use deceit and exploit emotion, and that their dupes are not armed to see through the impossible promises?

Is it the trouble with the "rootless leftist intelligentsia" that superficial education has killed simple faith and not provided the material for a more reasoned belief? Following Gurdjieff's leads, this writing has argued that the material does exist, to be found by looking as broadly as one can at the whole human scene past and present, inner and outer. The writing will keep running into sociology because current events provide so many object lessons of what happens in societies without a religious basis for ethics. Perhaps this implies that "a reasoned faith" would not be only about relations with the invisible, and personal life now and after death, but may seek responsible attitudes to our collective practical problems, population, resources, political power, violence. We can only hope the invisible power will help avert the most pressing dangers, but its methods seem to be to "reduce to absurdity" or "give them enough rope, they'll hang themselves", so crises continue.

Gurdjieff starts "***From the Author***" by describing the tasks he set himself to actualise, at first in theory and afterwards in practive, also by a means he had foreseen and prepared: namely by the first series of his writings "to corrode without mercy all the rubbish accumulated during the ages in human mentation"; by the second series to prepare "new constructional material"; and by means of the third to build a new world. That building will perhaps never be completed in Time and Space, but we could be helping it upward instead of destroying it, handing on material from which seekers can construct for themselves a house not built upon sand.

Letter from Grey received 28th October, 1974, "JESUS, FACT OR MYTH?" Jesus may be unhistorical but countless people have had the 'feeling' of a real person in the Gospels and of reality in his teaching." That is the devil of it, one revolts against having been deceived, and yet how much we owe to this religion and how much we need the feeling of an invisible friend who cares about every individual 'I'.

Mr. G is reported to have said in June 1949 that his dinners were forging unity to build a new world and fight the fake Jesus and God men have created; yet when he spoke or wrote of Jesus and other religious founders he did it with reverence. Surprisingly he stresses the importance of "information intentionally learned about real events which took place in the past" (**R.M.** pp 242, 243); one has come to feel he was referring to the birth of Christianity. Exactly what happened in that last century B.C. and first century A.D. it appears impossible to discover now, yet those who did know seem to have felt it a sacred duty to leave some clues in their works. That the new religion was launched with sacrifice and genuine inspiration one does believe.

If we are to look for some kind of Second Coming, as many in recent generations have felt, we are entitled to ask, what was the real nature of the Previous, or First, Coming? Or is there a continuous Coming to Individuals, unnoticed by the world? It could be that the figure of **Jesus**, friend, lover and beloved of souls, was created in memory of two S's, a Stephen and a Simon, who did give their lives in love of humanity, to help set up a new light and rallying point for those wandering in darkness. Probably elements for the life and character of Jesus were taken from Socrates, teacher and martyr, Asklepios the healer, Isis the compassionate, perhaps Spartacus the slave leader; and the mythical sons of Zeus, Heracles and Dionysus. It does not seem that a once-for-always sacrifice was enough. The light must be fed with oil, the redemptive stream kept flowing through the centuries by the efforts and sacrifices, imperfect as they are, of each generation. Perhaps this is why "all ancestors", the collectivity of the dead under a higher will, are felt to be active in our affairs.

* * * * * * *

PS. 25th May 1976. "Could be", but probably wasn't. Found a lot more.

V

POSTSCRIPT

1. Mr. Gurdjieff's Life

Various things suggest that Mr. Gurdjieff had medical training. It is reported that during Mr. Bennett's first 1948 visit to him in Paris, G said he had studied medicine and taken his degree, and that he had always kept his interest in medicine.

During a later conversation he told Mr. Bennett that he *was* at the Tiflis seminary at the same time as Stalin. Stalin was born 21st December 1879, and was at the seminary from age 14 till expelled (on 29th May 1899 according to a Soviet biography), because Marx's writings were found in his room.

Mr. Gurdjieff's date of birth is now given as 28th December 1877, so he was two years older than Stalin.

For him to change from a priestly to a medical training around 18 does not seem impossible but details would be welcome. It would appear that the "great being efforts" of his youth included intensive ordinary studying.

In "***God is my Adventure***", Rom Landau tells the story that G spent his "hidden years" in Tibet, nominally a Russian political agent. Mrs. Ethel Merston who lived a number of years at the Prieuré, evidently took this for granted as she said casually in conversation, "when the British wouldn't allow him to go back". "Where, when?" "To Tibet in 1911 with the Dalai Lama".

Fritz Peters in "***Boyhood with Gurdjieff***" makes us laugh with his stories of Miss Merston, "so English". This she was by education, at the Baker Street High or Canon Holland school, but her father had German Jewish origins and her mother, aristocratic Portuguese Jewish ones! Perhaps this is why she looked so splendid in a silk sari, though her warm everyday dress was a long Mexican poncho sewn down the sides.

It seems Mr. Gurdjieff's treatment worked for when she visited Coombe Springs in her seventies (1957) we found her a vivid and attractive person. She was still a gardener. During the war she became involved in social work in an Indian village near Benares, and left an interesting account of life there. Afterwards when not travelling, she had lived at the ashram of Ramana Maharshi, where she died in 1967. She shocked us hero-worshippers by declaring that Ramana was much more advanced than G. Perhaps G's psychology was a ''temporary building'', like the Prieuré's Study House, which was made from an old aeroplane hangar. By contrast, stone was used to build the Turkish bath-house.

She said she made the first English translation of Beelzebub, working with Mr. de Hartmann who turned the Russian into French. In the evenings the translation was read out to Mr. G, who made them find other words, with active or passive endings, although he knew hardly any English. Orage (1873 – 1934) to whom the translation is credited, only started it and then gave advice; he was in fact in America much of the time during Mr. Gurdjieff's writing years, running groups and collecting funds.

She told of a pilgrim march from the Himalayas which Mr. G taught – prostration, draw knees up, get up, down again – while saying ''I-wish-me-to-remember-the-self''. She thought the translation ''I wish to remember myself'' was wrong. Perhaps the self is not mine. She never heard of any complaints of sleeplessness at the Prieuré. They would even fall asleep at meals. When Lady Rothermere came to lunch G made a great story about cooking home-caught trout for her; they were perfectly good herrings.

Why did G disguise the account of parts of his early life? One reason could be that these stories convey better what were really adventures of the mind.

The diagrams Mr. Gurdjieff gave with the first version of his teaching, recorded by Ouspensky in ''***In Search of the Miraculous***'', leave the impression of a universe of great complexity, not to be easily grasped by the ''formatory apparatus''.

In all the diagrams: Ray of Creation, Laws of Worlds 3 to 96,

Cosmoses, the Hieroglyph of Life or Step diagram, there is the idea of many levels. Ouspensky gives 'The Three Octaves of Radiation' and the derivation from it of the first series of 'hydrogen' numbers with the upper levels of matter or energies, finer or less dense than those known to science, He does not publish the evocative names which the steps have in this version called 'Winds, Waves and Rocks', transmitted by J.G. Bennett.

2. Winds, Waves and Rocks

Do	The Absolute		
Si	Creation	H6	The Absolute Creator
La	The Absolute as Creator		
Sol	The Union of Three Forces	H12	The Law of Three
Fa	Six Triads (All Laws)		
–	The Great Creation (All Worlds)	H24	The Great Creation
Mi	The Laws of the Universe		
Re	All Suns	H48	The Sun
Do	Unmanifested Sun, Point 6		
Si	The Sun	H96	The Sun's Creation
La	The Heavenly Host		
Sol	Planets	H192	The Angelic World
Fa	The Inner Circle of Humanity		
–	Organic Life	H384	Organic Life
Mi	The Laws of Nature		
Re	Winds, Waves and Rocks	H768	The Life of the Earth
Do	Unmanifested Earth		
Si	The Earth	H1,536	The Earth
La	Elementals		
Sol	Good Karma	H3,072	Good Karma
Fa	Mechanical Aspect of Organic Life		
–	Mechanicalness	H6,144	Mechanicalness
Mi	Evil Karma		
Re	The Moon	H12,288	The Moon
Do	Absolute Nothing		

One copy adds "The Recording Angel" to Karma. What would happen if people really thought that a Recorder was taping all their talking and thinking?

3. *Notes from Mr. de Hartmann's Talk at Colet Gardens*

Notes by a non-musician of Mr. de Hartmann's talk at Colet Gardens on 9th March 1950. He was a short round man, he played for a joint A and B movements class.

"He gave an imitation of how we wriggle and scratch after a movement stops – the devil always finds something for us – but we must remain quite still after a movement till one more note gives the signal to move. 'This will make a big impression on your audience– and on you if you watch some day'.

He gathered us together and said: 'I tell once for ever about beginning of the music of Georgi Ivanovitch. In 1917 M. and Mme Ouspensky and others did movements, but 1918 was the beginning of music. Georgi Ivanovitch lay on a sofa at Essentuki with a guitar – but he did not strike it the ordinary way – and gave the melodies. There was a violin, he told me, 'In two days you must play it', so I had to: and 'a plate for putting glasses on' as a drum. (See his book, "***Our Life with Mr. Gurdjieff***" 1964 page 34).

Then in Tiflis we had a piano. Georgi Ivanovitch could do the impossible. In the midst of revolution he was working intensively on each one of us, our inner psychic states. It was a terrible piano. He said: 'Any idiot can play on a good piano', so I had to play on it. (See p 86).

When he wanted to make me angry, he gave the melodies each time a little different; he was training me. With these melodies there is only one right way to harmonize them, you have to 'catch' what they need. It is not 'my music'. it is his. I have only picked up the Master's handkerchief. Mme Salzmann remembers that time.

All the movements have their own scales. No. 19 is the five tone scale of Bali. The Chinese and Tibetan scale is different. Some have to be like "Little Bells" that hang in the temples.

The music and movements are one, they are like the body and soul in man, the rhythm is what joins them. You do not move in jerks on hearing the sound, like electric bells or lamps flicking up, but feel it beforehand. It is like a circle going round all the time, but as it passes a tangent touching a certain point, the actual movement comes'' He drew a big circle in the air with his right arm, brushing the left hand each time it passed.

''Those who had the great happiness to live with Georgi Ivanovitch know that something was given them, more than they deserved. He was trying to hammer a soul into man, something that could survive. Perhaps he is present here in reality.''

4. Conversation with Gurdjieff

Found at last, the account of Denis Saurat's conversation with G on a visit to the Prieuré in February 1923, given by Louis Pauwels in ''**Mr. Gurdjieff**''.

''What results are you trying to obtain here?''

'Better health, wider intelligence and a complete break with people's normal routine.'

'Have you already obtained your objective with some people?'

'Yes, in four or five years some of the disciples have reached the goal.'

'Do you know that several amongst them are near to despair?'

'Yes, there is something sinister in this house and that is necessary.'

'What is the object of all this manual labour and must it go on for long?'

'To make them masters of the external world. It is only a temporary phase.'

'Are you trying to give them occult powers?'

'I am trying to give them all powers. There is no difference between occult powers and other powers. The occultists today are all wrong. ...I want to create a type of sage who will unite the spirit of the East with Western techniques'.''

Pauwels also gives Katherine Mansfield's letters from the Prieuré to her husband, with some precious descriptions. Watching in the kitchen: "Madame Ostrovsky the head walks about like a queen exactly. She's extremely beautiful. She wears an old raincoat." (She was Mr. Gurdjieff's wife).

He reproduced Georgette Leblanc's account which was quoted earlier from memory.

* * * * * * *

5. *Advice of Grandmother*

"A good man loves father and mother. Then when they die, God will enter into that empty place."

Dorothy Caruso asked G "All these people (his regular pupils) have got a soul, why haven't I got a soul?" ...."Inwardly you are rabbit", he told her; she wondered how he knew...."You must work for your father". "But where is he?", "In the air, all around you". (From memory, her book was out of print).

At a meal in his flat (1948 or 49) Mr. Gurdjieff called for "advice of grandmother". "Or do nothing, just go to school, or do something no-one else does", Mme Salzmann repeated musically. Afterwards someone gave an explanation which seemed unnecessary then but stuck in memory: "By Grandmother he means All Ancestors". Finding herself unable to do as others did, the writer followed the encouraging Advice willy-nilly.

There is an invocation of G's beginning, "O Ye Holy Higher Forces, and Immortal Spirits of our Ancestors ...." Mr. Bennett told that he once asked in Turkish, "When can you get help from Higher Levels?" G said, "When you cry Amman, (Mercy)."

23.7.78. Proofreading. Go, book, on your adventures. May your nudity meet gentleness.

24.7.78. Bob Whiffen, its chief architect, said of our nine-sided Djami at Coombe Springs, that the building had a will of its own. Alas, all sacrificed, even the stained glass windows.

POSTSCRIPT

This is not "my book". It just grew. Far too much further draft is accumulating. "Going to school" in ancient literature has found surprising "inexactitudes". Life sentence.